For A Time
We Were Titans

For A Time We Were Titans

Tom Reed

iUniverse, Inc.
New York Lincoln Shanghai

For A Time We Were Titans

Copyright © 2007 by Thomas B. Reed

All rights reserved. No part of this book may be used or reproduced by any means, graphic, electronic, or mechanical, including photocopying, recording, taping or by any information storage retrieval system without the written permission of the publisher except in the case of brief quotations embodied in critical articles and reviews.

iUniverse books may be ordered through booksellers or by contacting:

iUniverse
2021 Pine Lake Road, Suite 100
Lincoln, NE 68512
www.iuniverse.com
1-800-Authors (1-800-288-4677)

The views expressed in this work are solely those of the author and do not necessarily reflect the views of the publisher, and the publisher hereby disclaims any responsibility for them.

ISBN-13: 978-0-595-42372-9 (pbk)
ISBN-13: 978-0-595-86708-0 (ebk)
ISBN-10: 0-595-42372-8 (pbk)
ISBN-10: 0-595-86708-1 (ebk)

Printed in the United States of America

For a time we were Titans. When we were new we fought beside giants and learned their ways. Later, as time and fate took the giants from our midst and we were thrust into their place, others, who were themselves then new, took us to be of the same metal as our mentors. This book is dedicated to the LRPs that fought in Vietnam. They struggled valiantly to preserve the freedom of a people half a world away and though the wider war was not won, the LRPs regularly brought honor to their units, their flag, and their cause. They were truly titans. But most of all it is dedicated to those LRPs whose names appear on the wall of honor, because they gave all they had. Men like …

Dickey Wayne Finley
Luther Ghahate
Gerald Hancock
Ralph Gerald Dunn
Hugh Rufus McKinney
Jack Lee Rightmyer
Barry D Murphy
Armin Blake
Steve Hathaway.

Contents

Foreword..ix
Prologue...1
Chapter 1   LRP..5
Chapter 2   Friendly Fire...............................12
Chapter 3   Friends Gained..............................18
Chapter 4   Friends Lost................................25
Chapter 5   What Happened?..............................35
Chapter 6   In the Field Again..........................39
Chapter 7   The Field Hospital at Nha Trang.............44
Chapter 8   Back to Bam Me Thuot........................48
Chapter 9   Firebase Mary Lou...........................53
Chapter 10 Conflict Between Brothers...................61
Chapter 11 Contact?....................................66
Chapter 12 The Holidays 1968...........................80
Chapter 13 The New Year................................89
Chapter 14 A Jug of Wine and a Cow.....................92
Chapter 15 Festus Runs into Trouble....................98
Chapter 16 Neugard Gets his Nose Pierced..............100
Chapter 17 What a Deal!...............................105

Chapter 18	The Giants Are All Gone	108
Chapter 19	Tac-E	112
Chapter 20	The LRP That Cried Wolf	118
Chapter 21	Lookout	124
Chapter 22	A Bronze Star for Massoletti	129
Chapter 23	The Ones That Got Away	134
Chapter 24	Ambush	140
Chapter 25	Hotel Two Alpha	147
Chapter 26	Final Mission	155
Epilogue		163

Foreword

The events described in this book are true, the people are real. But the author's memory has faded over the last thirty-seven years and in some cases details and names have been forgotten. In those cases I have invented new names for those individuals and I admit to a small amount of creative license in recreating the hazy memory of the some of the scenes described herein. In other instances names have been changed because I had to tell some stories that are unflattering to some of the men involved and I truly believe that we have all grown over the years and weaknesses that we exhibited in that long ago theater of war have been atoned for in the years that have passed.

I would like to thank Larry Massoletti and Warren Galleon for the pictures in this book, and I would also like to thank the LRPs with whom I served for their many years of friendship.

Jefferson City, Missouri November 22, 2006.

Prologue

◆

Remembrances Six Years Afterward

Monday, May 5, 1975

Dear Diary,

The news isn't good from the war front. It all started with the South Vietnamese retreat from Bam Me Thout. They said it was only a tactical retreat. But I know enough about the Vietnamese mindset to know that a retreat, any retreat, meant that the signs were against you, and you don't take action when the signs are against you. They retreated all the way to Saigon, and now the North Vietnamese are at the gates of the city, poised to finally conquer their southern brothers.

I have a speech tonight at the toastmasters Club. I'm going to tell them about the Vietnam that I know, about the LRPs, about the war we fought. I hope I do the LRPs justice, I want to honor them. They gave so much ...

It wasn't a large gathering at the Toastmasters that night. But the ones I wanted there were present; the members that were veterans. The ones who were Toastmasters were mostly World War II veterans, but one was a veteran of World War I.

When I was introduced I rose and walked to the podium. I acknowledged the toastmaster and my audience, took the manuscript from my pocket and then began to speak.

"It all happened a fifth of my lifetime ago. I was younger then, my hair was less thin and my waistline less broad. To be sure time has dimmed the memories of much that happened—but much remains. And despite how much I've changed, I know that those changes are miniscule when compared to the changes in the lives of the people I knew who lived there; the people of Vietnam.

"I remember well the people, their land, their war, and the Americans, too, who fought with them and for them; often not knowing why, but only knowing that they were called and that their duty was to answer that call. What is happening there now, the immanent collapse of all we fought for or to prevent; the demise of their clumsy, faltering, maybe futile, attempt at democracy; the loss of territorial integrity; their conquest by those who rule through tyranny and fear; and, the first unmistakable signs and reports of impending blood bath; what is happening there now brings those dimly illuminated memories leaping from my subconscious to my conscious mind.

"The Vietnamese are a gentle people, unlikely candidates to have withstood the rigors of twenty odd years of war, small, almost miniature in stature, with a tendency toward cleanliness and neatness that belies the filth of the battlefield or the rubble of bombarded cities. The big and brash American GI could never become used to seeing two Vietnamese boys, both soldiers, comrades in arms, holding hands as they walked down a city street or along a country road. The immodest American could never grasp the modesty that caused a Vietnamese male to bathe wearing a loin cloth while his sister a few yards down stream bared and bathed her breasts. The lusty and robust American could not understand why the Vietnamese resented a playful roughing of their hair or a jocular patting of their cheek. We did not understand their culture, their taboos, their mores, and all too often, because we did not understand them, we did not respect them.

"This is not to say that as a people they were without faults. By our standards, they were often ruthless in their quest for money. There were no goods, no services, no vices, that they would not provide the American GI provided the price was right. I cannot say for certain that this was their nature, that it was born in them. Perhaps, their greed was born of the insatiable appetite of the American soldier. Perhaps it is inevitable that where our armies go, a basically good and gentle people are perverted.

"The people of Vietnam that I grew to know and like the most were the Montagnard tribesmen of the Central Highlands. Remnants of their primitive innocence that they knew before the years of war could still be detected when I was there. Unlike the Vietnamese, there was no charge for their friendship. If you were a guest in their village you were treated like royalty, what was theirs was yours, while, at the same time, what was ours was safe from encroachment by them. In my entire life I have never met a more honest, a more reliable, a more courageous group of people. I am saddened by the thought that these people, Vietnamese and Montagnards alike, who have for the last two decades withstood the ravages of war, should find the peace they long dreamed about, to be a peace without freedom, a peace without independence.

"Also, from a personal standpoint, I am saddened that now that the bamboo curtain is descending over Southeast Asia, I will never again see what I consider to be the most beautiful country on earth. From the white sand beaches of Cam Rahn Bay and Vung Tau to the triple canopy rain forest of the Central highlands, Vietnam is a veritable paradise. I spent most of my time there in the Central Highlands, in Pleiku and Kontum Provinces, in jungles teeming with exotic wildlife and rugged mountain foothills accented with clear flowing rivers that wold occasionally plummet over waterfalls into translucent pools below. There has been much said about the ravages of war on the landscape of Vietnam, of defoliated trees and fields pockmarked with bomb craters. I cannot deny that this is so, but the jungle has remarkable recuperative powers and the scars are not long obvious. Within weeks of an attack of bombs and defoliants the deadened leaves are overshadowed by new lush greenery sprouting from the jungle undergrowth and the bomb craters are hidden by the broad blades of elephant grass which tower fifteen or twenty feet from the crater pits. Stories of Shangri-La and tropical paradises are written about places such as this.

"Now, as with China and Korea, as with the steppes of the Ukraine and the tobacco and cane fields of Cuba, those lush rain forests and rugged waterfalls of Vietnam will disappear from the view of all but a select few of the western world, veiled by an alien philosophy and the distrust inherent after more than two decades of war. It is sad ..."

1

LRP

Monday October 14, 1968

Dear Diary,

Our arrival in Ban Me Thuot was like a scene from Greek myth. As we walked into the LRP[1] cantonment the earth quaked beneath our feet and the starry sky was rent with peals of unholy thunder. But it was not the wrath of ancient gods that greeted us; it was that of modern man reaching out for an unseen enemy. It was the booming of 175-millimeter Howitzers that shook the earth beneath us, and made it seem as if we were lifted off the ground with every step we took.

We were FNGs, fucking new guys, straight out of the replacement depot at Camp Enari in Pleiku. There were ten of us: Torres, Jackson, Jordan, Carter, Stotler, Hardy, Slusarz, Neugard, Murphy and me.

I should give you their first names and Army rank, but most of the time I didn't even know their first names. We never used first names in Vietnam, you were either known by your last name or a nickname, like Festus, or Cueball, or Cookie. As for rank, you usually wore your rank, for the benefit of any lifers that were around, but among the LRPs it didn't mean anything. For the most part everybody was treated alike. Oh, there were some things, like guard duty and policing the area, that noncoms got out of but for the most part three stripers got treated just the same as Spec Fours and Privates.

Officers, of course, were always called by their rank and name, but among enlisted LRPs the only exception to the unwritten rule on rank was the Platoon Sergeant. He was almost always a Sergeant First Class and a career soldier. The

---

1. LRP pronounced Lerp stands for Long Range Patrol.

men knew that the Platoon Sergeant was the glue that held a LRP platoon together and they gave him the deference of his rank. Unless you were really close it was Sergeant Blake, Sergeant Hinkle, or Sergeant Hooper. (But, at least with one of them, across the poker table, or over a beer in the Bunker Bar, it was just "Hink.")

It was the guy who was then Platoon Sergeant, Sgt. Blake that recruited us into the LRPs. He came to Pleiku, to the Fourth Infantry Division Replacement Center, called the Repo. Depot. This is where you had to go to get FNGs to replace troops that had gone home, or for that matter, those that would never go home. He was there, specifically, to augment the Second Brigade LRR platoon. The authorized strength of the platoon, the number of GIs the brass in the pentagon said should be in a platoon, was too few to do all that needed to be done.

An Army Division is divided into three Brigades. Each Brigade in the 4th Division had a LRP Platoon At the Division level they had a whole LRP Company. It was officially Echo Company, 58th Infantry, and it providing three more LRP platoons. But, E-58th was never at full strength, except on paper. To build up the brigade units they would borrow from Echo 58th. So, in truth, Sgt. Blake was recruiting for Echo 58th, although he knew the FNGs he recruited would go to 2nd Brigade.

Blake was an impressive figure, a dark complexioned bull of a man dressed in camouflaged jungle fatigues, and with a felt Australian bush hat set squarely on his head. "I want to tell youse about the Lerps," he told the FNGs that showed up to hear his spiel. "Lerp is L—R-P. It stands for Long Range Patrol.

"Our job is to go out in four or five man teams and find the enemy. Hopefully, we find them without them finding us. Now, youse guys may want to ask why any damn fool would want to do that, when you can have a platoon of thirty-five guys around you? Or when, if you go with a track unit, you could have a nice APC to travel in, and you don't got to walk? Well, think about it. APCs make a lot of noise going through the jungle. So do any platoon of grunts. They got steel helmets banging the brush, rifles hitting against ammo bandoleers, and guys talking at the top of their lungs. We don't do that. Lerps keep quiet. We don't talk above a whisper when we're out there, we tape down, or button down all metal that would bang against somethin' else, we don't wear steel helmets, we wear boonie hats instead, and we walk slow and quiet. There is an advantage to small numbers; you don't make as big a target.

"There are other advantages too," he said. "General Westmoreland says that after youse guys run twenty-five missions you can go back to base camp, and take a cushy job for the rest of your tour. And besides that, instead of the usual one in country and one out of country R and R, as a Lerp you'll get two out of country R and Rs and one in country R and R."

It was not the most articulate pitch I had ever heard, but still Sgt. Blake had struck a cord. Shortly before I had washed out of Officers Candidate School, with full knowledge that I would be headed for Vietnam as a regular grunt, I began thinking about the type war I wanted to fight. Marching through the jungle with a platoon of men that were making more noise than tin cans being drug behind a newly weds car, didn't appeal to me. I liked the idea of small team missions. In fact I wanted to be a LRP even before I knew what one was. I filled out the paperwork and gave it to Sgt. Blake.

A day or two later when Sgt. Blake had had a chance to check out our records, he was back. My turn to see him came in the late morning. I was nervous. I didn't think that I would be anxious to get into any army unit, but I really wanted to be a LRP. When I entered Sgt. Blake started talking without any preliminaries.

"We'll catch a flight from here to Ban Me Thout. We don't have enough camouflaged fatigues right now but in a little while ..."

I interrupted him, he was talking like I was in, but he hadn't said so. "Does that mean I'm a Lerps," I blurted out.

"Oh, hell yeah," he said. "I looked at the test you took when you joined up. We ain't never got nobody with scores like yours before."

So that's how I got to the 2nd Brigade LRPs at Ban Me Thuot.

Every other firebase that I've ever heard of had a name, but if the firebase we were on had one I never heard it, or if I did, I've long since forgotten it. It was simply known by the same name as the Vietnamese city it was near. Ban Me Thuot is in Darlac Province, in the Central Highlands of Vietnam. The areas status as hill country must have been only in comparison with the Delta farther south. It was pretty flat. There were a few low rolling hills but they didn't seem very impressive, even when compared to the Ozark foothills where I had been raised. There was jungle here and there, really little more than little patches of woods but there were also large open plains. The firebase was in the middle of one of those plains. You could smell the Plains. It wasn't particularly rich soil, but there was a lot of it. The grass gave off a clean herbal smell that to some extent countered the earthiness of the soil.

Our official address was Headquarters Company, 2nd Brigade, LRP Platoon, APO San Francisco 26262, but where we lived was a small cantonment on the Northwest corner of that unnamed firebase. Three rows of tents and a small L shaped parade ground was the heart of the LRP area. The two rows of tents housed the enlisted men and faced a dirt road from one side. The headquarters tent, supply tent and armory faced the road from the opposite side. I was given a cot in the back of the first tent in the second row.

The FNGs had gotten to know each other back in Pleiku, and for the most part we stuck together, at least at first. Of the guys I came in with, I most often hung out with Neugard, Murphy and Torres. I guess that I was tightest with Murphy.

It was pretty easy to tell who was old and who was new. The new guys wore standard army issue olive drab jungle fatigues. The real LRPs wore camouflage fatigues called either Trees or Tigers. The Trees were loose fitting army issue fatigues that were mottled in shades of green, brown and tan. Tigers came through the black market, or by trading with South Vietnamese or Korean outfits. They were tight fitting and had slashes of black interspersed amid splotches of green.

Among the first things the FNGs were given were olive drab, canvas Australian Bush Hats. The brims buttoned to the crown on the right side and lay flat on the left. Throughout Vietnam they were generally know as LRP hats. They were like a badge; we wore them everywhere, with the exception of when we were on a mission. Sgt. Blake's was the only bush hat made from felt.

The first few days were pretty much getting acquainted time. Missions were being run, but the new guys weren't melded into the teams right away. They did have us do some army stuff. Things like walking guard duty. We were too green to be trusted to guard the perimeter, but were entrusted to guard spots like the motor pool that were inside the camp perimeter. That way we would less likely to screw up and let the V.C. overrun the place. For the most part though we just sat around waiting and talking.

The first real LRP that I got to know was Shaner. He was the assistant Platoon Sergeant. It was his job to see that we were equipped and settled. He was a good-looking guy with fair skin and reddish brown hair. Prescription sunglasses almost always hid his eyes; he'd lost his regular glasses while getting away from a bunch of bad guys. For some reason he took a liking to me, and took me under his wing.

"I don't run missions anymore," he told me. "Haven't run any for about a month now. This is my second tour, and I've got something over forty missions behind me."

"I thought you only had to run twenty-five missions?" I asked.

"They didn't make that rule until I was already well passed twenty-five. Some guys just keep running missions anyway. You get pumped up out there, especially when there are VC or NVA around. Old Festus probably has more than fifty missions and he hasn't quit."

"Why did you quit?"

He looked down and shook his head as if he were trying to clear it of the thoughts and visions that were in it. All he said was, "You know when it's time."

After a day or two, Sgt. Blake decided to take us out to zero in the weapons we had been issued. Some of the established LRPs came with us just for the practice, or just to get out of camp. All the FNGs had M-16s. Many of the LRPs that had been there a while carried shortened versions of the M-16 called Commando AR-15s, or more commonly, CAR-15s. One of these established LRPs, Adams, brought along a rifle he had just modified. It was an M-14, the rifle that had been the standard infantry weapon before the M-16. He had cut the stock off at the pistol grip, and shortened the barrel to the length of the gas piston. The whole weapon was no more than 18 inches long.

When the duce and a half[2] we were riding in reached our destination the first thing I noticed was that it wasn't a rifle range. It was the camp dump. We were going to zero in our rifles on tin cans and empty bottles.

It was as if I was back on the farm again, plinking tin cans with my Winchester 22 pump. I don't want it to sound like I was raised in the back woods and had to hunt to put food on the table. Our farm was only two miles from town, and our food came from the supermarket, but I had been shooting a rifle since I was seven or eight. For a while, when I was in my teens, we raised pigs. Rats would dig under the concrete slab of the pig house, so that they could dart into the pig house at night to feed on the corn the pigs left behind. I honed my skills with a rifle by running water down one rat hole, and shooting them when they popped their heads out of another.

I was having no problem hitting the cans and bottles I aimed at on the first shot. The fact was, the area we were in was too small to present much of a challenge. None of our targets were more than fifteen or twenty yards away. I decided to make the target practice a little more challenging, and lowered the rifle to my hip. I chose as my target an empty can about five yards away. I didn't notice that Adams had raised his sawed off rifle, and with careful aim down the barrel was honing in on the same target.

We fired at the same time. The can jumped into the air at an angle indicating that the effective shot had been mine. The LRPs around Adams had been concentrating on his shooting, and were unaware that two shots had been fired. They

---

2. A Duce and a half is a two and one-half ton military truck.

began to congratulate him on his marvelous shot. Only Neugard had clearly seen that it had been my hit. He started to come to the defense of my shooting accuracy, but I raised my finger to my lips in a sign to keep quiet. My grin told him that it was our secret, and that I thought it not a good idea to begin our relationship with guys that had earned their tiger fatigues, with an argument over shooting prowess.

When we got back to base the first thing we had to do was to clean our weapons before turning them in to the armory. I was sitting on a wall of sandbags in front of my tent cleaning my rifle when Shaner came by.

"How did the target practice go?" He asked.

"Pretty good," I said, "but you couldn't get any shots over twenty or twenty-five yards."

"Well you probably won't get many shots at a greater distance when you get out into the jungle either."

I guess I looked confused.

"Those jungles can get pretty thick. There will be sometimes when you can't see five or ten yards."

"I noticed that some of the guys carry rifles other than the M-16 or CAR-15."

"You don't like the M-16?"

"I'd like something a bit more heft, something not as likely to rise up on full automatic."

"I know what you mean," Shaner said. "Some of the guys like different weapons for different reasons. I guess you saw Adams' sawed off jobbie. Miller carries an M-14 too, but he hasn't sawed his off. Hell, I've even seen him go out of here with a bayonet stuck on the end of it. I've known other guys who carry shotguns loaded with buckshot. I didn't carry an M-16 either."

"What did you carry?"

"I carried a M-60 machine gun. I wanted to be able to lay down a pattern of fire without having to change magazines every three seconds. Like you, I also wanted something with more punch than that 5.56 they load into the M-16."

"A machine gun can eat up a lot of ammunition, how did you carry enough ammunition to keep an M-60 fed?"

"I carried a couple of belts of ammunition wrapped over my shoulders. The other guys on the team carried additional belts."

"How do you get something better than an M-16?" I asked.

"Well you can bet the Army's not going to give you anything else, maybe a M-79 Grenade launcher, but that's only good as a secondary weapon. You still need something that's capable of firing on fully automatic. You've just got to keep your eyes open and watch for opportunities to make a trade."

"Well, I guess I'll just have to do that."

"Until then you'll just have to put up with the M-16, starting tomorrow."

"Tomorrow?"

"Tomorrow you guys are going out with Festus. He's taking you on a training mission."

"All right!" I said.

"I don't know about that," Shaner said. "Festus is tough, but ten FNGs might just put him over the edge."

2

Friendly Fire

Wednesday, October 16, 1968

Dear Diary,

Tomorrow we go out on a practice mission. I guess I'll get my first taste of the jungles around here. I know it's just a practice mission but still I am a bit nervous. I know it's not a real mission. We aren't going in by helicopter, we are walking. The place we're going is a patch of jungle less than a kilometer away from here.

We drew our weapons and ammunition from the armory. The armory wasn't really a building, or even a tent, it was a large steel shipping crate called a Conex, protected from enemy fire by sandbags on three sides and the top. We were now ready to set out.

"Damn," I heard Murphy's voice behind me.

"What's wrong?" I asked.

"Look at this," he said thrusting out the grenade launcher he held in his hand.

"It's an M-79,"[1] I said. "Every team carries one with them."

"It's a fucking single shot," he said. "I don't want to carry this damn thing."

"It don't mean nothing," I said taking the M-79 from his hand and giving him my M-16. "We're just going for a walk in the woods." We headed out from the firebase in single file, across the open fields and toward the tree line.

Festus' real name was Gibson, but everybody called him Festus because of his resemblance to the character in the TV show <u>Gunsmoke</u>. The resemblance was strongest after he came in from a mission with a five day growth of beard,

---

1. The M-79 looks and operates like a sawed off single barrel shotgun but fires a 40 mm high explosive round, a smoke marker round, or a canister round of buckshot.

unkempt hair and sweat soaked fatigues. With more missions than any active LRP, he was a legend even among the giants.

When we reached the tree line we stopped, and Festus gathered us around him.

"Now, when you leave your helicopter the first thing you do is head for the tree line," he said in a soft southern drawl. "Once inside the tree line you stop and lay dog. There will be four or five of you out there and you'll all be looking in different directions. There's no rule about how long you stay in that location. Maybe twenty minutes, maybe two hours. You just want to be sure that no enemy saw your insertion, and if they did, you want them coming after you while you're in a defensive position. You don't want to walk into them when they're set up in an ambush, and you want to be close to the landing zone. There will be times when you make contact in the middle of the jungle, and have to hightail it to a LZ, but anytime you can set up close to a landing zone you're that much closer to a safe extraction.

"Laying dog is also when the Team Leader, or RTO[2] if the Team Leader lets him, will establish commo with the radio operator at S-2[3] back at the fire base." He crooked his finger for the guy who was carrying the radio to come to him. "The RTO always walks right behind the Team Leader." He reached around the RTO and took the handset from his pack raised it to his ear and mouth, broke squelch and spoke. "Seven Niner Charley, this is Two Alpha, over." He listened.

He completed the commo check then replaced the handset in the top of the RTO's pack.

"Now we're going to head out here, and you're going to take turns walking point, carrying the radio, and walking rear security. From here on we're going to move like a Lerp team. You don't talk unless you have to, and then only in a whisper. Most of my commands will be by hand signal. We're going to walk slow, and we're going to walk quiet. Watch where you put your feet, I don't want any twigs snapping. Watch the jungle on both sides. You," he pointed at Neugard, "You're first on point. You," he pointed at me, "you're rear security."

We moved out, into the jungle. The trees were not exceptionally tall. The underbrush seemed thin. I had been in many woods back in Missouri that were more rugged. In time I would find other jungles, jungles where the trees towered to the sky and the underbrush stifled my movement, but this jungle was an

---

2. RTO—Radio Telephone Operator.
3. S-2 is the Brigade Intelligence Officer (usually a Major) and his staff.

almost civilized jungle, too close to towns and villages to be truly wild. It seemed too close to man, to be close to nature.

I didn't recognize that nature is not the enemy. Throughout the millenniums man have learned to coexist with nature, and often, as with this patch of jungle, to pervert it to his ways. In time I would come to realize that I was safer in a true jungle, with all that is wild, the wild vegetation and the wild animals than in a jungle too well populated by the human animal.

We moved on. Every thirty or forty minutes we would stop, set up, and just listen. Then, in five or ten minutes we would alternate the point man, and the guy who had been point man moved to rear security. In that way I was slowly moving up the line toward point. It was still in the fore noon, I had moved up two or three spots, when ahead of us I could see the jungle thin out, where we were about to emerge into an open field. It was then that we heard the shot, and the snapping of the broken branch above our heads. The branch fell among the leaves at our feet.

"Get down!" Festus ordered and we all sunk to the jungle floor. "Bring me the grenade launcher," he said in a horse whisper.

I made my way in a low crouch to the front of the line and handed him the grenade launcher. At the other side of the clearing, about a hundred and fifty yards away, was a small hut. He broke open the breach. "Give me the grenades," he said.

"Oh, shit," I said, "I didn't get those." Still maintaining the low crouch I made my way back to Murphy. "Give me the grenades," I said. He handed over the bandoleer, and I took it to Festus.

He loaded a round and closed the breach. 'Phoomph,' the slow moving projectile was on its way. It moved at the speed of a well hit baseball, you could follow its' trajectory throughout its' flight. It hit the ground, and exploded a few yards from the hut. He repeated his actions, and the second shot was even closer. Before he could fire again a white flag appeared from the door of the hut.

He handed me the M-79 and picked up his CAR-15. He just looked at me, and shook his head. I couldn't have been more embarrassed had he chewed me out in front of the whole group.

Two figures approached us from the other end of the field waving a white handkerchief hung from the barrel of a rifle. As they got closer we saw that the taller of the two was in a South Vietnamese uniform. The shorter was a boy of thirteen or fourteen years. We kept our weapons pointed at them until they reached our location. Festus reached out and grabbed the rifle from the fellow's hand.

"Why were you shooting at us?" he asked.

"Not shoot at you," the fellow in our allies uniform said. "Shoot at birds. Not see you."

"Well I didn't see any birds," Festus said.

The Vietnamese put his wrists together and flapped his fingers imitating a bird in flight. "Me shoot at bird," He said. He looked to his companion for confirmation. The younger Vietnamese just nodded his head.

"Shoot birds, take to Village, eat," the older one said trying to make us understand that they were no threat."

Festus motioned for the RTO to come forward. He took the handset from the pack and spoke into it.

"Seven Niner Charlie, this is Two Alpha, over." He listened to the response, broke squelch and spoke again. "We've come under fire, and captured the guys that were shooting at us. One is about twenty, the other is a kid. The older one is dressed in an ARVN uniform, and was carrying an M-1 Carbine. He said they were shooting at birds, but the shot was to close to our heads for comfort. There aren't any birds either. Do you want us to bring them in for questioning?" He listened again then spoke to us.

"He's going to check with the officer of the day." In a few minutes those of us who were close heard the radio's muffled voice.

"Two Alpha, Seven Niner Charley, Over."

Festus listened. "Roger, out," he said. He pulled the magazine from the carbine and jacked back the bolt to extract the round that was in the chamber, then handed the rifle back to the Vietnamese soldier. He tossed the magazine to the boy. "You can go now," he said, "but don't reload that thing till you're a long way from us." The older Vietnamese bobbed his head in obeisance then the two walked quickly away in the direction from which they had come.

"Okay, let's move out," Festus said the disgust in his voice only slightly less than before. As I moved back to my place in line I paused at Murphy, gave him back the M-79, and took back the M-16 for which I had ammunition.

The next time we took a break we ate our LRP rations. We learned to heat the water in our canteen cups using flammable blue tablets in a stove made from a C-Ration can. We poured the boiling water over our dehydrated rations, and let them sit for five minutes. Even then the crunch was not totally gone from my beef stew but I was hungry, and truly enjoyed this new kind of rations. The others seemed equally rapt in their consumption of chicken stew, pork and scalloped potatoes, chili con carne and spaghetti in meat sauce.

After our meal we were on the move again. It may have been about thirteen hundred hours when we came to a small village of five, or six thatched roofed, bamboo huts. Chickens pecked their way around the village, but there were no humans to be found. Some of the men wanted to set fire to the huts, sure that the village must be a hot bed of Viet Cong activity. They argued how easy it would be to set fire to low hanging eaves of the grass roofs.

"Seven Niner Charley, Two Alpha, over." Festus said into the radio. Seven Niner Charlie's response took longer than the normal radio salutation. The look of disgust again darkened Festus' features. "Now S-2 wants to interview our prisoners," he said to us. He broke squelch and again talked into the handset. "Isn't it a bit late for that? You told us to let them go two hours ago. They could be miles from here by now, over." He waited while Seven Niner Charley took the information to the Major.

"Well, you can tell him that I'm disappointed too. That's why I called it in the first place. Now, why I called you this time. We've got a small village here that's inhabited by nothing but chickens. Do you have anything on it? Wait a minute; I'll give you the coordinates." He checked his map and scratched some numbers in a small notebook. Then he took his code book and translated the numbers into the military alphabet. "We're at delta, foxtrot, Juliet, bravo, alpha by bravo, November, delta, echo, golf."

There was again a prolonged silence. "Roger, out," he said finally. "For all they know this is a peaceful Montagnard village. If we burn it down they might decide that they like the V.C. more than they do us."

Eventually, it came to my turn to walk point. It was by then late afternoon. The shadows were becoming long on the trail. In the jungle they fell like a bizarre arabesque, occasional splashes of sunlight and shade weaving intricate designs but giving off no recognizable shape.

I took up my position, now armed with a loaded M-16 rather than an empty M-79. I don't know if Festus knew that I had spent the first half of the day carrying an empty weapon for which I had no ammunition, or If he thought I had taken the M-79 from another team member and brought it to him while we were under fire, but didn't have sense enough to bring the ammunition with it. He didn't broach the subject, and I didn't tell him which kind of fool I was. He told me to follow the trail we were on, to maintain a slow steady pace, and mainly, to keep my eyes open.

Nobody who went to Vietnam did so without hearing the horror stories of what happened to guys who walked point; about the click you heard the moment before the land mine you stepped on exploded. About pungy stakes that the enemy pissed on so that you would get an infection after you stepped on one. About hitting a trip wire and releasing a grenade from a booby trap or coming face to face with a V.C. when you rounded a curve. You couldn't take up that position for the first time without some trepidation. Little did I know that there would come a time when I would lead my own team, and trust no one else to walk point, when I wouldn't believe that anyone else could read the signs that the trail had been tampered with. But booby traps and pungy pits were rare occurrences. We walked the same trails the enemy trod, and they didn't often booby trap where they themselves might be the victims.

The fact that we had come under fire, even though it appeared to be friendly fire, had taught me that in Vietnam there was no such thing as just a walk in the woods. We were at war, at any time you could be under fire.

Even had Festus not told me to keep my eyes open, I was now very alert to all that was going on around me. When I saw it, I stopped immediately. It was five or six yards ahead of us, a slithery black line that spanned the trail from side to side. Its' head and tail were hidden by the underbrush, but it was clearly a cobra, a cobra of impressive size. I canted my head toward Festus without taking my eye off the snake. "Do you want to take this native back to the Major for questioning?" I whispered, "or do we just call in an air strike on him?"

"I think we can let this one go, too," he whispered in reply. The snake seemed to sense our presence, the undulations suddenly became more pronounced as he streaked across the trail, and into the underbrush beyond.

We got back to the firebase in time for supper in the mess tent.

3

Friends Gained

Thursday October 18, 1968

Dear Diary,

Tomorrow I go out on my first real mission. Looks like I've got one hell of a Team Leader too. He looks like he could beat a NVA platoon all by himself ...

Can you tell the quality of someone just by looking at him? Can you see their strength? Can you read their integrity? I think you can. It's not just amorous love you can feel at first sight. Sometimes, even among men, normal men, there can be a fraternal love at first sight. Sometimes you can just look at someone, someone you've never seen before, and know you want them for a friend ... So it would be with each of the men I would meet this day. I could tell their strengths, I could tell their integrity, I knew I wanted them for friends.

"Are you Reed?" A giant filled the doorway of my tent.

There hadn't been much to do. I didn't have any duties, and was too new to have earned a pass into Bam Me Thuot. So it was mid-morning, and I was lying on my cot reading a book. Then I heard the deep voice and looked up to see the figure of a huge black man in the doorway. His black hair was short and curly, his face, like every thing else about him, was strong. I was reasonably tall, close to six feet, but he towered over me by several inches. And I wasn't puny, pushing 200 pounds, but he had me by twenty or thirty pounds. And there wasn't any fat on him either. Calling him a giant wasn't just figurative, he was big.

"Yes, I'm Reed."

"I'm Colbray," he said. "You're on my team. We're going out tomorrow, and you're going to be my RTO. The birds are scheduled for eleven hundred hours.

We'll draw our equipment at zero nine hundred." With that he was gone. He was all business. I was impressed. If all team leaders were like him, guys like me were going to have a hard time measuring up.

I closed the book and got up. I was feeling that combination of thrill and apprehension that comes from facing the unknown, yet knowing that it is an unknown that you have yourself invited. Colbray had in his few words given me all the information I needed, but not all that I wanted. I wandered across to the headquarters tent where I knew the teams would be posted.

When I entered I found Shaner sitting at a small table perusing some papers. "What ya up to?" he asked looking up from his work.

"I just found out I'm going out tomorrow."

"Yeah, you're going out with Colbray." He nodded his head toward the chalk board where the teams were posted. The teams were listed under their call signs. I scanned the team leaders name until I found Colbray under Two Delta. Beside his name were the letters TL for team leader. Under his name were listed Murphy and the letters ATL for Assistant Team Leader. My name was next with RTO after it. The fourth and last name was Torres. So the team was to be made up of three FNGs, and a very large black man who looked as if could have the other three of us for lunch any time he chose.

"What do you know about Colbray?" I asked.

"For one thing he's strong as an ox. He came from a line unit a few months ago. A little while back Miller got sick while he was on a mission. I think he had a touch of malaria. Well, anyway, they ran into some bad guys and it got a bit hot. Miller called for extraction the chopper that went to pick him up had already picked up Colbray's team. The pilot couldn't land the chopper because of brush in the LZ so it was hovering a few feet off the ground. Miller's team got on all right but he was too weak to climb on the skids. That's when Colbray reaches down and grabs Miller's web belt with one hand and braces himself against the floor of the chopper with the other. He just picks Miller up with one hand and hauls him on board."

"I don't think I would want to make him mad at me," I said grinning.

"That's not likely," Shaner said. "He's pretty easy going."

"Thank God for that. So we're going with a four man rather than a five man team." I said changing the subject.

"Two Alpha and Two Bravo are five man teams. Some Lerp units run six to eight man teams, but the Fourth Division has always run four or five man teams. We don't have enough guys for six man teams and we can only put out two five man teams. Why do you ask, do you think you need an extra guy to do the job?"

"It seems logical that five sets of eyes, and five guns are better than four," I said.

"It's also one more man to make noise, and one more man to keep track of when you're trying to get away from the NVA," Shaner said. "I really prefer four man teams, and there are some times when even four are too many."

He read the questioning look on my face. "There have been a few times when we've run two man missions, and I've heard stories of some Lerps that go out alone."

"Two I can see, but if I went alone I'd like to have a Montagnard with me."

"Hey, Yards count. If you got a good one with you they're worth two Americans. I wish we had more of them with us. Right now we're down to just Chue and Doc. They're both good, especially Chue. But he's still healing from a wound he picked up on a mission a couple of months ago. Unlike us, they don't get to go home when they're shot. They're already home."

No matter how hard you try you can't stretch the time required to pack to fill the time left before departure. If you can stretch it to half an hour you're doing good. I started by surveying my equipment. I started with the pack itself. It was hung on an aluminum frame that helped distribute the weight evenly across your back and hips. The pack itself was nylon and, of course, olive drab. There were four canteen pouches, two pouches on each side, and a long pocket across the front in which you could carry small things. There was also a pocket in the pack's top flap for things you wanted to get to in a hurry.

Below the pack attached to the frame were two nylon straps to attach a rolled up poncho and poncho liner. The inside of the pack was deep and spacious. I tried to calculate how much room would be left when I put a PRC 25 radio, and extra battery inside. There seemed to be plenty of room, but I knew the radio would weigh about 25 pounds and I didn't want to overload the pack to where I couldn't move quickly if we got in trouble. I opened my foot locker to decide on the equipment I would take with me.

I'd heard that in World War II the thing guys wanted most in the field, was a pair of clean, dry sox. I held a pair in my hand for some time then tossed them back in the foot locker. We were only going to be out for four or five days so I decided that the pair I would put on in the morning would see me through. Some of the guys had told me that you didn't want to be too clean, you wanted to smell like a part of nature. They said that the VC could smell soap and after shave a hundred yards away. I figured that the same sox and underwear after five days in the jungle should make me funky enough to compete with any critter out there.

In the bottom of the footlocker I found the New Testament that the minister of my Church back home had given me. It was a standard King James Bible except that the cover had a steel plate built into it. I put it on top the pack so I could put it in my shirt pocket when I got dressed in the morning.

I tossed four packs of cigarettes into the pack. I would carry two or three more packs in the pockets of my jungle fatigues. There still wasn't much in the pack. There would be plenty of room for the radio, a Claymore mine and the eight or ten LRP Rations I would need. I looked at my watch. The packing had taken me eighteen minutes.

I sat back on my bunk and thought about the things that I might really need in a combat situation. There were some things that I didn't have that I really wanted. I wanted a hand gun, one that I could conceal and use in emergencies. I figured that I would have to get that in country; I had heard that they didn't allow personal hand guns to be shipped from the States. I also wanted, no, I really needed, a good knife. That I could probably get from home, I wasn't aware of any prohibition against mailing knives. I got some stationary and a pen from the footlocker, and wrote a letter to my brother. I asked him to try and find me a British Commando knife, like the one he had gotten from an army surplus store when he was about sixteen. We had both practiced throwing that knife, and had gotten quite good with it.

After dropping the letter in the mail box in the headquarters tent I went to the mess hall for lunch. After lunch I decided there was nothing else to do to prepare for the mission so I went back to my tent and my book. After supper I wandered into the party tent. Really, the party half tent. It was just the front part of one of the sleeping tents. One of the guys had a record player and a few records. The record that was usually playing was Simon and Garfuncle's album of music from the "Graduate." Every once in a while someone would put on Arlo Guthrie's "Alice's Restaurant." It seemed that the one thing we all had in common was going through the draft physical.

I never was much of a beer drinker. I don't dislike it, but I don't guzzle it either. I can nurse a can of beer for an hour or more. So after a couple of beers it was pretty well dark. The rest of the guys that were in the tent were more advanced in their partying than I was, and there were no empty chairs in the poker game so I wandered out into the night.

It was a beautiful night. I've always liked the night. The darkness always seemed like a shield giving you a protective invisibility. On this night the sky was filled with stars. The moon had not yet risen, so there was nothing to rival their brightness. The firebase was dark. If there were more lights they would only make us a better target. The men in the guard towers along the perimeter could see just fine without light. The brush was cut for a couple hundred yards around the base and mine fields and concertina wire filled the mowed area. Any bad guys that got in there would either be seen or would not escape the mine fields or barbed wire. The only lights there were seemed to drift from the open doors of the tents. I went to the parade ground to try to escape what lights there were. There was only one tent facing the parade ground, and the light from its entrance was dim. I gazed up at the sky wondering if these were the same stars I had so often seen at home. I had to stop and think if Vietnam was north or south of the equator. I pictured the globe in my mind. North I thought, just like at home, then in evidence of my conclusion I found the Big Dipper. I followed the stars in its' lip and found Polaris, marking the northern sky. Again I thought, just like home.

"Who's out there?" Even the accent of that voice reminded me of home.

"I was just admiring the stars," I said looking toward the tent, and seeing the questioner standing just outside the entrance.

"Well, don't worry about them, they ain't going no where. Come on in and have a drink with us."

I followed him into the tent. He was broad shouldered, about my height, and had light brown hair. At the other end of the tent a couple of cots were pulled up to serve as seats around a footlocker. On the footlocker was a half full bottle of bourbon, some paper cups, Coke cans and a coffee can filled with ice cubes. Sitting on one of the cots was another fellow shorter and darker than the one that had invited me in, but equally well built.

"While I was out taking a leak I found somebody to help us kill this bottle," said my guide. "By the way, who the hell are you?"

"Reed," I said.

"Well, Reed, sit down and have yourself a drink." He sat down at the other end of the cot his friend was occupying.

I put some ice in a cup and poured myself a double, then sat down.

"You want some Coke with that?"

"No thanks, I'll just let the ice melt a little. You know who I am, but I don't know who I'm drinking with."

"I'm Finley and this here," he said nodding his head toward his companion, "is Ghahate."

"Where are you guys from?" I asked.

"I'm from Missouri," Finley said. "Ghahate is a real live Indian from Arizona."

"What tribe?"

"Hopi," Ghahate said. I was half surprised that he answered, I was beginning to think that Finley did all the talking for both of them.

"You must have brought some talents that come in handy while Lerping."

"Yeah, we have lots of jungle on the reservation."

"Don't let him kid you," Finley said. "He's good. I'm glad to have him as my ATL."

"Where are you from in Missouri?" I asked Finley.

"A little town you've never heard of called Sweet Springs."

"You'd be surprised," I said. "It's on Highway 70 between Sedalia and Concordia."

"Damned if he doesn't even know where it is," Finley said.

"I used to go through Sweet Springs all the time when I was going to school in Warrensburg. I'm from a small town in east Missouri called Pacific."

"Well, you topped me," Finley said adding some whisky and Coke to his cup. "I never heard of that one."

"It's about thirty miles west of St. Louis."

"So you were a college boy, did you graduate?"

"Oh, yeah, I earned a Bachelors of Arts in Political Science; A degree that qualifies me to do nothing."

"It would qualify you to be an officer."

I took a long drink from my cup and added more ice and whisky. "That's what I thought when I signed up. Then I spent some time in OCS[1]. I found out that, not only isn't it worth an extra year in the Army to wear a gold bar, but that I don't think much of those that do wear them." A slight smile crossed Ghahate's lips but he said nothing.

"I've been told that the Marine Corps takes recruits in boot camp and tears down everything they were and rebuilds them the way they want them to be," I said. "That's the way the Army seems to approach their officers. I liked the way I was, so I fought the system."

"Did they kick you out?" Finley asked.

I had to chuckle at that. "That would have been too easy. I think they wanted to keep me in, so they could prolong the torture. But, after about ten weeks they accepted my resignation.

I took another drink of whiskey.

"That set you up to come here." Finley said.

---

1. OCS is Officers Candidate School.

"I was coming here either way. I have to admit, though, with all the pushups and extra laps they made me do, I was in the best shape in my life when I got out."

"Well, that's what's so amazing about being a Lerp," Finley said dividing the last of the Bourbon among our cups. "I'm a team leader and a PFC, and even if General Westmoreland was grounded with team Two Alpha, I'd be in charge. It makes you proud to be an American," he said raising his cup in a mock toast. We followed suit. "Have you been on any missions yet?"

"Just a training mission with Festus, and we got shot at by some South Vietnamese during that, or at least we think they were South Vietnamese."

"Sometimes it's hard to tell." This time it was Ghahate that spoke.

"When are you going out for real?" Finley asked.

"Tomorrow," I said. "I'm on Colbray's team."

"We're going out tomorrow, too. We'll have to do this again when we get back." We drained our cups, and I headed back to my tent ready to sleep and to face the adventure that awaited me in the morning.

4

Friends Lost

The passenger seats were folded up against the back wall of the helicopter. We sat on the floor with our backs against them. Actually it was our packs that were against the folded seats, as we would not take them off during the flight. It was a Bell UH 1, better known as a Huey. It had two large cargo doors that were slid back against the fuselage, and would remain open throughout the trip. As there were no seats, there were no seat belts. Once in the air there would be nothing between us and a fall to certain death, but a few feet of floor.

The ship had a crew of four. The pilot and co-pilot sat in the cockpit while the two door gunners sat on web seats and manned their M-60 machine guns. The guns were mounted in little niches in the back wall of the cabin, one on either side of the ship. The crew wore helmets with microphones attached so that they could communicate with each other. Our only means of talking to the crew once we were airborne would be to tap them on the shoulder, and shout above the noise of the rotors.

I had never been in a helicopter before. I wouldn't say I was scared, but I would have felt more secure if there had been something more to hang onto than an M-16. A minute or two after we took our places I saw the pilot move his right hand on the throttle and the rotors began to spin faster. The helicopter began to lift and, as more torque was applied, to move forward. Before long we were shooting across the ground, and gradually rising higher and higher into the air.

We had drawn our equipment at nine that morning as scheduled. We went first to the supply tent for our rations, and a PRC-25 radio. It came with an extra battery, hand set, and two antennas. I put the radio in my pack and screwed the short whip antenna into the top of the radio. The long antenna was in six or seven pieces wrapped by a rubber band. An elasticized string ran through the hollow length of each piece, and when you cast them out the pieces would pop together into one long unit that looked somewhat like a cane fishing pole. I attached the cord on the handset to the top of the radio, and attached the handset to a loop on the shoulder strap of my pack.

Colbray took a dozen LRP rations so the rest of us followed suit, and took an equal amount. We mixed them up to ensure a variety of the dehydrated meals. After loading the rations in our packs we went next door to the armory. There we drew our rifles, an M-79 (Murphy insisted on carrying it, along with his M-16), grenades and a Claymore mines, with electric wire and charging handle for each of us. The Claymores and their accoutrements also went into the packs. Three fragmentation grenades, two smoke grenades, a white phosphorus grenade, and a tear gas grenade went into canteen pouches, or the pockets of our jungle fatigues. We were then ready and departed for the helicopter pad.

Now we were in the air moving rapidly toward our designated area of operation. Colbray leaned in toward the rest of us. "When we touch down, we'll exit two on either side," he said. "The helicopter won't be on the ground for more than four or five seconds. When it takes off again you two," he pointed to Murphy and Torres, "come across to our side, and we'll head for the nearest trees. I want us all to have our feet on the skids when we start into the LZ."

It is hard to say how long we flew. The helicopter was a new and exhilarating experience, like your first roller coaster ride or the first time you took the family car out by yourself and found a lonely stretch of highway and pushed your foot to the floorboard. All too soon the helicopter began it's decent. We scooted toward the open door, and dropped our feet onto the skids. I watched the ground get closer and closer, and glancing ahead saw the tree line some seventy yards away.

The helicopter touched down. I don't think that more than the nose of the skids touched the ground. The moment that we jumped off, it rose again, skimming the top of the grass for a few tens of yards, and then climbing above the trees. It rose higher and higher, and moved farther and farther away into the distance.

We took off toward the tree line at a steady jog. When we reached it we dropped into crouches, and stared off into the jungle looking for the merest sign that our insertion had been compromised. Colbray's gaze was intense, nothing about him moved except his eyes.

After a minute Colbray appeared to breathe again. "Give me the hand set," he whispered. I unhooked it from my shoulder strap and handed it to him.

"Seven Niner Charlie this is Two Delta, over," he whispered into the mouth piece then a pause. "Commo check, over." And after another pause, "Roger, I hear you lima charley, too, out."

He handed back the hand set and whispered, "If we hit any trouble I'll switch packs with you, and carry the radio. That way I can call in artillery, or gun ships while we are on the move." We lay dog for only a few minutes until Colbray was convinced that our insertion had been clean. Then, we began to move.

And move we did. Colbray walked his own point, and with his long legs and muscular body, set a pace that was hard for mere mortals to maintain. I walked second, behind Colbray, Torres followed me and, Murphy walked rear security. I would have cursed my luck at having to carry the extra weight of the radio but ahead of me, on Colbray's back was a pack that was filled beyond it's maximum capacity. The pack was stretched till it appeared about to burst, and the exterior pockets bulging out from the body of the pack were so stuffed as to resemble the statue of an ancient fertility goddess. To top it all Colbray didn't use an aluminum pack frame to distribute the weight. The entire hundred pounds or more, that I estimated was in that pack, was carried across his broad shoulders. I hoped we wouldn't run into trouble—not because I feared confrontation with the enemy, but because I feared that if I had to carry that pack very far that it would be too much for my mere 6 foot, 200 pound body.

When I glanced behind me I saw Torres and Murphy struggling to keep up. Torres was the shortest one on the team, and he had his head down and was walking as fast as his short legs could carry him. It was lucky that the ground was hard and dry because Murphy didn't have time to cover our trail. It was all he could do to keep up, and occasionally turn around to make sure no one was following us.

We had been going at this rate for close to an hour when the trail we were on ran into a broader one, following along the bank of a small river. Another five minutes on this trail, and we came upon a Montagnard village. Unlike the village we had found on our training mission, this one was full of life. Women and old people sat around the doors of the huts doing those chores that kept their lives together, and half naked children of every age and size, seemed to be everywhere. The adults paid us little attention, but as soon as the children saw us they ran to us, and seemed to form a line paralleling our march jabbering at us in Pidgin English. All I could make of what they said was the "hey, GI."

"No, no, no can do," Colbray was saying back to them. "Maybe later we come back."

"What do they want?" Torres asked in a whisper.

"You don't need to whisper," Colbray said, "they know we're here. They want us to go fishing with them."

"Fishing," I said, "why do they want us to go fishing?"

"Because we've got hand grenades," he said. "If a grenade goes off in the river the shock waves go out in ripples, and the concussion knocks out all the fish for ten or fifteen yards. They come floating to the top, then all the kids have to do is wade in and pick them up."

By now we had passed the last hut in the village and the children, looking somewhat dejected, watched us go on our way. When we were some way away from the village we stopped for lunch. LRP rations were broken out and prepared. I tried the beef stew. The little chunks of meat didn't totally re-hydrated in the five minutes that we let them sit before digging in and were consequently a little stringy. But the vegetables were soft, and the gravy was pretty good. For dessert I had a jungle chocolate bar. It had something added to it to keep it from melting in the tropical heat, so it didn't taste much like a real Hershey Bar, but the mornings hard walk had made me hungry, and it tasted just fine. I topped off the meal with a couple of the Lucky Strikes from the four-pack that was packed in with the meal. I would save the Salems I had packed for later. When we finished, we dug a shallow hole with Colbray's K-Bar knife and buried the empty packages.

After lunch we left the trail and headed out across the grass lands, and through sparse patches of jungle. We moved almost constantly taking only two five minute breaks. We didn't stop until late that afternoon. When we stopped it was at the head of a small patch of jungle close to an open area large enough to serve as a LZ if we needed extraction.

"We'll stop here till it's almost dark," Colbray explained, "then we'll move into our night location."

We sat and listened. We didn't talk much. Torres and I smoked a bit, the other two didn't smoke. I was sorry I hadn't brought a book. Some people get so absorbed in what they're reading that they don't know what's going on around them, but I had always been able to read and still be aware of my surroundings. Then I remembered I did have something to read, the Bible in my breast pocket. I took it out and read. Colbray leaned back on his pack and chewed on some beef jerky someone had sent him from the States. Torres smoked another cigarette and Murphy just sat and listened. After a while one by one we would get out a LRP Ration, prepare it and eat. As we had at lunch, we borrowed Colbray's knife, and buried the trash.

As dusk settled around us and it was becoming difficult to read, Colbray sat up. "Okay, now it's safe to go into our night location," he whispered.

He led us to a thicket that was in the LZ, but only a few yards from the jungle. On his hands and knees he cut away a few stems with his knife, and made a passage just big enough for us to crawl through. The ground on the interior was mostly clear but, we did have to cut away a few stems to give us enough room to lay out our bedrolls and lie down. Colbray told us to lay out our bedrolls in a square, so that who ever was on watch could reach out and shake any member of the team if there was any trouble. The location was cramped but totally hidden from anyone that might pass by.

Once we were set up Colbray had us unpack our Claymores, and set them out to cover all four sides of the thicket. We crawled through the interior of the thicket being careful to disturb as few stems as possible. We set the Claymores at the edges, being careful to ensure that both the front and back blast were pointed away from our hiding place. Then we plugged in the cords, and stretched the wire back to where we had started. We placed the charging handles beside our packs. We were now ready if we had any nocturnal intruders.

We sat cross legged for a while talking in low whispers. We talked about home, about girlfriends or wives, about what we would do when our tour of duty was over, the normal things that G.I.s talk about. Then one and then another of us would stretch out on our ponchos. Then one, and then another would rest his head on his pack, and then one and then another would pull his poncho liner over him. Finally only Colbray was still sitting cross legged. "We'll stand watch in two hour shifts," he said, while he still had an audience that was awake. "I'll go first, then Murphy your next, then Torres and then Reed. Reed, as soon as the sun is up you call in the sunshine report."

Our world grew silent with the only noise being the rustling of leaves in the night air. At first the silence was broken only by the scurrying of some small animals in the nearby jungle. Then, all at once there was a far off chattering, an irregular staccato barking with the rapidity of a machine gun. Since I had been in Vietnam I had heard about the distinctive sound of the AK-47 assault rifle that armed our enemies. I raised myself on an elbow.

"Is that an AK-47?" I whispered.

Colbray listened silently for a moment. "I don't hear nothing but the chattering of those damn monkeys," he said. I lay back down and was soon asleep.

The next sensation I had of a hand slightly shaking my pants leg. "Hey man, it's your turn on watch," Torres whispered.

I raised up on an elbow and rubbed the sleep out of my eyes. "Okay, I'm awake," I said. I sat up and crossed my legs. I knew better than to try to stay awake while in a prone position.

The moon had set and the night was pitch black. Only a few stars could be seen between the leaves of the brush above my head. Shaner had showed me how you could smoke at night without the flame of the match or the lighted tip of the cigarette being seen. I wrapped the poncho around me, overlapping the edges then ducked my head beneath the folds and lit a cigarette in the darkness of this personal tent. Then I raised my head above the folds, carefully keeping the cigarette cupped in my hands beneath the folds of the poncho. I couldn't keep my head under very long or I would be choked by the buildup of smoke. Shaner told me that I could do the same thing with just the poncho liner, but I would have to double it over, or it would light up like an lantern. Every few seconds I would cover my mouth with the tent, and take another drag.

Watch is a lonely time. Everyone else is asleep and you're left with only your thoughts for company. For the first few minutes you think about how important it is to stay awake. Then once you are fully awake you experience the full spectrum of thoughts of any wakeful man in the dark of night. But, mostly you think about war, and you think about peace. You think about what you would do if you heard the noise, or saw the movement that you most feared. How you would reach out your hand and shake each team member in sequence, and whisper the word "movement." How you would then reach down and pick up your rife, and then reach out with your other hand and pick up the charging handle of your Claymore. You rehearse these actions in your mind again and again.

Then when you have gone through the process for what seemed like an infinite number of times, your mind wanders and you begin to think of peace, and of home. You think, what would I be doing if I were at home right now? You think about what you are going to do when you get home. You think about the girl you loved, about the job you left, or the career you had chosen.

Slowly, but eventually, the blackness of the night turns more and more gray, and then the first glimmers of light appear in the sky. The jungle begins to stir once more. Birds that were silent through the night begin to sing their morning songs, and the small night hunters are heard skittering back to their dens. I picked up the handset broke squelch and made our sunshine report. A new day has begun.

The second day of the mission was much like the first. We walked and walked at Colbray's pace. The area of operation was only four square kilometers, and I was amazed that we hadn't crossed our own path at least once. Colbray seemed to be winding his way back and forth intent on covering every square meter of the AO. That night we made our night location in the jungle about 30 meters from an open field that could serve as a LZ. The night location was protected by fallen trees on two sides and thick undergrowth on the other two.

The third day started much the same as the second but by mid morning we came across a new wrinkle in the topography. It was a large open field, but unlike the others it had not been grazed by Montagnard cattle, and water buffalo. Here the grass was tall enough to even tower over Colbray. It was thick too, not the breadth of the leaves, it was not like the elephant grass that I would find farther north, it was the number of blades growing close together that created the thickness.

We waded into the grass pushing down an easy to follow trail. I glanced back at Murphy. He tried to cover our trail behind us, but there was no way he could lift up all the broken and trampled blades to hide our path. In a little while he abandoned the effort and rushed to catch up with the rest of us. We had walked quietly in the jungle, and quietly in the shorter grasses of other fields, but this tall grass was dry and rustled noisily as we moved through it.

It was near the middle of the field that I first noticed that the rustling seemed to grow louder. Colbray must have noticed it too, for at first he slowed and then he stopped, raising his hand as a signal for us to stop as well. The noise didn't stop. It was coming at us from the other end of the field.

"Fan out," Colbray said in a low whisper, signaling with a wave of his M-16 that we were to cover both sides of our trail. Murphy and I covered the right and Torres the left. The noise came closer and closer. Colbray held his M-16 tight against his hip. The noise was no more than five yards away.

"Now!" he shouted. He began raking the grass with M-16 fire, and the rest of us followed suit.

When his magazine was spent Colbray took out a hand grenade, pulled the pin and lobbed it in the direction of the noise. "Let's go!" he shouted, and led us back down the trail we had just made. In the eight seconds it took for the grenade to explode we were safely away from the blast area. Murphy emptied a couple more magazines covering our retreat.

When we reached the tree line Colbray stopped. "Switch packs with me," he said. Even with my adrenaline pumping the weight of Colbray's huge pack staggered me. It was even heavier than I had imagined, but I took my place in line, and managed to keep up, albeit walking a bit more stooped that before. We continued to retrace our steps with Colbray whispering into the handset.

There we no signs that we were being followed. No shots had been fired back at us. But there had definitely been something moving in the grass. It could have been one or more human beings, possibly Vietcong or North Vietnamese, maybe not. It could have been a water buffalo, or a tiger. It, or they could now be dead or wounded. We didn't know, and it didn't appear that we were going to go back to find out.

In about 15 minutes Colbray halted our movement. He replaced the handset in the shoulder strap loop, and removed the pack. "Murphy, you see any signs of anything behind us?"

"No, nothing."

I happily relieved myself of the burden of Colbray's pack. "What have you got in there, an anvil?" I asked.

"I was a grunt before I joined the Lerps. When you're a grunt you carry everything you own with you. I never got out of the habit."

"You must own a lot of stuff," I said.

"They're not going to pull us out," Colbray said lifting his own pack back onto his shoulders. "The Major said that if we didn't see them, and they didn't shoot at us there was no reason for an extraction." He looked around and checked his map. "We might as well take a break here."

I had not yet put my pack on, so I reached down and took a canteen from its compartment. I shook it, it was nearly empty.

"We're all running short of water," Colbray said. He glanced back at his map. "There should be a blue line[1] down there," he said pointing toward the bottom of the ridge that we were on. "Murphy, you and Reed go down and get us some water."

We each took six of the empty canteens and our rifles and headed down the hill. Sure enough a small creek ran through the valley at the bottom of the ridge. With a couple of minutes search we found a pool deep enough to dip our canteens. When the canteens were full we headed back up hill. It was steep enough that the trip up was much more difficult than the descent. We had to move further down the hillside to find an easier climb, and still, in a couple of places, we had to grab hold of small bushes that rustled as we climbed, and at least once a small stone broke loose and tumbled noisily down the hill.

Then, a burst of automatic fire. The trees above our heads threw splinters down on us. "What the hell!" I said flattening myself against the hill. The shots had come from the area where we had started.

"Is that you guys?" Torres voice said from above us.

"Torres, stop shooting at us!" Murphy shouted.

"Hey man, I didn't know it was you."

---

1. Blue line—For the line on a map that indicates a river or stream.

We completed our climb and emerged on the ridge huffing and puffing. "Damn it, Torres! The enemy doesn't shoot at us but you do," Murphy said.

"I heard movement down there. I thought you guys were farther that way," he said pointing toward the way we went down.

"When you're climbing a hill you don't always come up the same way you went down," I said handing Torres his canteens.

That night we made our night location just inside the tree line only a few feet from a LZ. I had second watch that night, following Murphy who was in the lead off spot. At 23 hundred hours I felt his hand shaking me awake. When I sat up and rubbed the sleep from my eyes, I could see his outline in the darkness. He had the handset to his ear.

"One of our teams has movement," he whispered.

"Whose team?" I asked

"I don't know who it is. His call sign is Two Alpha."

"That's Finley," I said. "I had a few drinks with him and his ATL the night before we left."

"Well, they've got flashlights coming real close to their night location." He handed me the handset and lay back down on his bedding. I lifted the handset to my ear and listened. At first I heard nothing, then the voice of Seven Niner Charlie broke the silence.

"Roger, Two Alpha you say a dozen or more flashlights? Over." There was silence. Two Alpha was too far away to be picked up even with the long antenna that was on the radio.

"How far are the flashlights from your location? Over." Again there was silence.

"That's too close for an air strike or Spooky[2]. I can get artillery for you, over."

"Roger, I'll hold off, over."

"Roger, out," Seven Niner Charley said. Evidently Finley had terminated the transmission. I kept one ear to the handset, and the other listening to the little world around our night location. Our vulnerability was becoming clear to me. The bad guys could as easily been looking for us as for Finley. The lack of information from the radio made me nervous for my new found friends. Finally, maybe a half an hour after the last transmission the radio crackled alive again.

"Roger, Two Alpha, I understand you have blown your Claymores and are evacuating your current location. Wilco, on the choppers." A few more minutes

---

2. Spooky was a C-47 (DC 3) airplane made into a platform for miniguns. Earlier it was called Puff the Magic Dragon.

of silence passed as BTOC, the Brigade Tactical Operations Center arranged for the extraction helicopters.

"Two Alpha, Seven Niner Charlie, the choppers have been scrambled," Seven Niner Charlie said finally. "What is your current location? Over."

"Roger, the ETA for the birds will be approximately 30 minutes, over."

I looked at the luminous dial on my wristwatch. My two hours on watch had ended ten minutes before. I wanted to stay awake and listen but knew it would be at least a half hour before we heard anything else. I needed sleep if I were to be effective in the morning. I shook Torres awake and briefed him on what was happening to Finley. I handed him the hand set and lay back down. The worry about my friends should have forestalled sleep, but exhaustion won out, and sooner than I would have expected I was again asleep.

When I awoke it was daylight. Only Colbray was awake. He was heating water for coffee.

"What happened to Finley's team?" I asked.

Colbray looked over at me. "Three of them got on board the chopper," he said. "Finley and Ghahate never made it."

5

What Happened?

Monday October 22, 1968

Dear Diary,

So this is what it's like to lose friends. I've lost family, my father and grandfather. I was four years old when my father died. That was so long ago I don't remember how I felt. I was seventeen when my grandfather died, but he was nearly ninety and had cancer. He was suffering. It was almost a blessing when he died. But Finley and Ghahate were young and still had a lot to live for …

It was mid afternoon when we were finally extracted. We'd been on the move most of the morning and early afternoon, and hadn't been able to pick up even the scanty information offered by our radio. As soon as the helicopter landed at the firebase we headed for the headquarters tent. Shaner was just coming out as we arrived.

"What happened?" I asked, pulling off my pack and dropping it at my feet.

"Ghahate is dead. They're still looking for Finley," he said in response to my question. "The gooks knew they were in the area and came looking for them. They reported seeing flashlights all around them. They didn't want to call in artillery because they were afraid it would only confirm that the gooks were close to finding them. When the gooks got too close, and it was obvious they were going to be discovered they blew their Claymores, shot up a few magazines and got the hell out of there.

"They headed for a small river, and waited there for the helicopters to arrive. They kept shooting up their ammunition to keep the gooks at bay. By the time the birds arrived they were out of ammunition. Finley taped his strobe light to his long antenna, and Ghahate used it to direct the birds to where they were, while Finley talked them in.

"To have enough room for the blades to miss the overhanging tree limbs the extraction ship had to come down in the middle of the river. The team waded out to where they were. They were in about two feet of water and the skids were maybe another two feet over the water. Finley and Ghahate helped the other team members get onto the skids then threw their rifles on board.

"Here the story gets garbled. The pilot and co-pilot say that our guys told them to take off, our guys say it was one of the door gunners, and the door gunners say that nobody told the pilot to take off, he just did. I heard that the crew had been partying before the mission, and were still drunk. But, it didn't matter who did what or why, the fact was the chopper took off, and Finley and Ghahate were still on the ground. One of them, evidently Ghahate, grabbed hold of the skids. One of our guys looked over and saw somebody hanging there, but in the dark, he couldn't tell who it was. Our guys shouted at the pilot to go back that they didn't have the whole team on board, but by that time they were more than a klick away from where they had left Finley. When our guys looked down again the skid was empty.

"They turned the chopper around but couldn't find the spot on the river where it all happened. They searched for about an hour, and then gave up. There was no way Finley could contact the chopper. He didn't have a radio, he couldn't use his mirror or smoke at night. If he had a strobe light or signal flares, he may have thought the gooks were too close to risk using it. After all, he was alone and unarmed, his rifle was on board the chopper.

"Back here, once we knew they were coming back with only part of the team, we called for volunteers to hunt for Finley and Ghahate. Every Lerp that was here volunteered to help. I was real proud of them. All they needed to know was that brother Lerps were in trouble, and they were ready to go.

"In the end, they decided not to use our guys. It was a line company that found Ghahate's body. He had been wounded. They couldn't tell if he had been shot off the skids, or if his wound had occurred before, and had weakened him enough that he couldn't hang on. They haven't found Finley yet, but I heard that they found a strobe light, and a Bible stuck in the fork of a tree. He may have left it as a signal that he was about to be captured. They're still looking, I hope, I pray they'll find him."

"What was the call sign of that chopper crew?" Colbray asked.

"I don't know, it was Stagecoach something. Why?" Shaner said.

"If I ever get in any trouble," Colbray said, "send somebody else."

We turned in our gear and headed back to our tents. I needed a shower, shave, clean clothes, and a toothbrush. I gathered my stuff and headed for the showers. Murphy was there ahead of me, and as there was only one shower head. I had to wait until he was finished.

"I never even knew them," he said over the noise of the splashing water.

"I barely did," I said.

"But you liked them?"

"Yeah, I really did," I said lighting a cigarette. "Ghahate didn't talk much, but you got the feeling that you could depend on him, that if you were ever in trouble he'd be there. Finley was," I had to stop and think of the words I wanted to describe him, "a good old country boy," I finally said. "The kind of guy who would stop to give you a hand if you were broken down on the road. In fact, he could probably fix your car on the spot, and wouldn't take any money when he was through. Capable, but not flashy." I had to stop again and choose my words. "He was home, Murphy, or at least my only link to it over here. He was the type guy I went all through school with. Never the class valedictorian, but not dumb either. He wouldn't date the prom queen, or a cheerleader, and he wouldn't be elected most likely to succeed, or most popular, but everybody would like him, and he would have succeeded. He wouldn't have been the president of a big company, but he might have had his own gas station or soda shop. He wouldn't have been elected to Congress, but he might have been Mayor of Sweet Springs."

"Yeah, I guess I know what you mean." Murphy had finished showering and was toweling off. "I guess I would have liked them too."

I put out my cigarette, finished undressing and got under the shower. Murphy left without saying anything else. I emerged some twenty minutes later, clean, shaved and with the residue of four days worth of dehydrated food scraped from my mouth. Torres was just arriving.

"Hey, man, you use all the hot water?"

"There wasn't any hot when I got here, but there's a whole lot of tepid."

"What's that?"

"Warm, Torres, warm."

Finley was never found. His name remained on the platoon roster posted in the headquarters tent with the letters MIA beside it. The only thing that changed was his rank. By the time I left the 2nd Brigade LRPs in July, 1969 he had been promoted, in absentia, to Sergeant. Ten years later, in 1978, his status was changed to killed in action.

I went back to my tent and put away my things. I lay down on my bunk. I was bone tired, but I couldn't sleep. I eyed the book I had been reading, but I didn't want to read either. There was nothing I wanted to do. I had always been very independent, and self confident, but now the reality of my mortality had come down hard on me. I had always been at home where ever I was, but a tie to my real home had been found, and now I had lost it. I had always liked being alone with my thoughts, with no one to bother me, but now, for the first time in my life, I was lonely.

6

In the Field Again

Saturday October 26, 1968

Dear Diary,

I'm going out on another mission this morning. It will be mostly the same team as last time, but we've got a different Team Leader ...

I guess I should have been leery about it. The three FNGs had screwed up enough that if the bad guys that we saw behind every bush had really been there we would have been in deep trouble. I'll never know what we encountered in the grass, but I don't think we handled it very well. And Finley's team proved that there was a lot of danger out there.

But I still believed in what we were doing in the LRP way of fighting. I just hoped that I was on an upward learning curve. I thought to myself, this time I won't be so dumb. This time I'll act more like a LRP.

Miller was our team leader. He was not a giant in stature, like Colbray, but was one in experience and ability. The AO was completely different than the AOs I'd been in with Festus and Colbray. The rest of the team was the same as it had been with Colbray.

The jungles were a little thicker, but most of the land was still open grasslands. The grass here was long, maybe waist deep, but far shorter than the tall grass I had encountered with Colbray. There were no villages in this AO, at least none that had been inhabited in some time. In fact, there were no signs of living human beings, only the dead.

We found a Montagnard grave yard. It was nearly buried by the grass, but gradually as we moved the grass aside, we found the statues. Strange wooden carvings intricate in detail, and in their way, primitive works of art. They were enclosed by rail fences to keep the domestic, if not the wild, animals at bay.

With each mission and each new team leader I learned something new. From Festus I'd learned the basics. From Colbray the art of cutting out the inside of a thicket to construct a near perfect hiding place. Now, from Miller I learned that finding the enemy, not necessarily killing him, was the goal.

"Sometimes you make contact," he said one night, "nearly every Lerp makes contact once in a while, but when you do it's a mistake. When you make contact, by definition, the enemy knows you're there. The idea is to get in, find the enemy, and get out without being discovered. Then the Division can send in an infantry unit, tanks, a B-52 strike or whatever it takes to wipe them out."

Miller practiced what he preached. He walked his own point, and moved almost continually, always searching for signs of the enemy, but unlike Colbray, he moved slowly, careful to make as little noise as possible. He avoided trails, choosing instead to parallel them through the jungle. Where Colbray marched boldly, Miller moved stealthily. I imagined that this must have been the way that Ghahate would have moved, like an Indian in the forest, cautiously, persistently, and silently.

During one of our stops I asked him about his M-14.

"I don't trust the M-16's," he said. "If I shoot at something I want to knock it down, not just shoot through it. I carry a tracer in my chamber. I always thought that I had better see where the first shot goes before I shoot again. The last 2 shots in the magazine are also tracers, that way I will get a warning that I need to change magazines."

On this mission, I began to hone the skills I would use most often during my first six months, and eighteen missions as a LRP. Here, I first assumed the position of rear security.

When I told him I was going to walk rear security Shaner had told me about the value of the positions.

He said, "The most important position on a team that was on the move was point. The point man controlled the pace and direction of the movement." I found it interesting that Both Colbray and Miller walked point as team leaders, but Festus did not, he would walk closely behind the point man, and when needed, whisper directions.

"Second in importance to the point man is rear security," Shaner had said. "Rear security had to make sure that the team was not followed, and was responsible for concealing the team's trail. You can't always erase the signs that the team had been through an area, but you could disguise them. You could raise a few feet of trampled grass where the path entered an open field, and weave trampled strands into the grasses on either side. You could drag limbs across the path, limbs the enemy would presume to have been broken by human passage. You could brush away foot prints in dust and sand. You do all that you could do to make your passage as hard to detect as possible," Shaner had told me. But what he forgot to mention and what I found out on my mission with Miller was that you had to do all that while not letting yourself get to far behind the rest of the team.

As rear security I also started carrying the M-79 grenade launcher. It was almost always carried by rear security. I'm sure that there was a theory as to why it was best carried by the man at the rear of the team, but I couldn't tell you what it is. I, as did most others that carried one, always carried it as a secondary weapon. It was very effective for dropping an exploding round amid the enemy, but was useless for laying down a pattern of fire.

The mission ended with a great deal learned, but the only intelligence that was gained was that the bad guys were not in that AO. Back at the firebase between missions I did fulfill one of my equipment goals. For the outlay of $150 I was able to obtain a used Ruger 22 caliber automatic pistol that new, would have cost half that price in the United States. But in Vietnam hand guns came at a premium. The only problem was that the seller had no 22 ammunition. I soon found out that no one else in Bam me Thuot had any either. I was told that if I could get to a Special Forces Base, they had almost every type of ammunition known to man. In the meantime, the pistol would have to remain in my footlocker.

My next mission was again with Festus. The Brigade was planning a move and they wanted to make sure that a couple of areas were clear of enemy activity before we left. Therefore, Festus, the most experienced team leader, was to take out an eight man team to cover the area of greatest concern. Eight men were pretty much the limit for a team that could be transported by helicopter.

On this mission we again proved the negative. There were no enemy troops in the Area of Operations. But one thing happened to me on this mission that would reoccur much later in my tour of duty.

We slept on the ground in the jungle. The floor of the jungle is crawling with insect life. Termites, and red ants are ubiquitous but no real threat to sleeping GIs, but centipedes were a different story. These are shelled worms with multiple pairs of legs all along their underbelly, and a sting that you couldn't feel, but that would turn your legs to jelly, and give you hives that would itch like crazy. On the last night of this mission I was the victim of such a critter.

As I was already laying down I did not realize the weakness in my legs, but I could feel the bumps that covered my body, and I wanted to tear off my skin to rid myself of the itch. I didn't get much sleep that night, but by dawn the effects had worn off, and the hives abated. I did not equate the miserable night I had spent with the hard shelled worms I had seen in the night location, at least not then.

Months later, when I had my own team I set up an ambush along a trail that showed evidence of recent travel. We hid Claymores close to the trail and crawled into the undergrowth where we couldn't be seen. In that underbrush were several centipedes. I didn't pay them much attention, as I hadn't related my earlier sickness to their presence. Within two or three hours of our stakeout I started to itch.

The effects were even stronger than my first encounter. I may have been stung by more than one. I was so ill that I decided there was nothing to do but ask for an emergency extraction. I called in and reported my symptoms, and requested extraction. I did not say I had been stung by one, or more centipedes because I was still unaware that they were responsible for my mysterious illness. The team packed up and we headed out to find a landing zone. I was so weak that after only a few hundred meters, I had to give up my pack to another team member. I stumbled along totally reliant on the rest of the team to lead me to safety. We found a bomb crater big enough to serve as a LZ, and with some effort I encoded the coordinates and called them in. It was then that the Lieutenant told me that we were not to be extracted.

I don't know how I survived that night, but I did. When you can't sleep because of the terrible itching you search your mind for the cause of your malady. Gradually you put two and two together, I remembered the mission with Festus months earlier, when I had had similar symptoms. My minds eye reviewed the conditions of that night location, and compared them with my ambush site. It was then that I realized that centipedes were present at both locations. The culprit was recognized.

The day that dawned was the last day of the scheduled mission. I was still weak when we were extracted, and flown back to Mary Lou. The Platoon Executive Officer was sitting in the passenger seat of the jeep that was waiting for us at the helicopter pad. We threw our packs, and weapons into the jeep's trailer and climbed in the back of the jeep.

"Well I see you're alive," the Lieutenant said. "You mustn't have been as sick as you thought you were."

"I'm still a little weak, but I figured out what caused it," I said.

"Oh, yeah," said the Lieutenant.

"The place where we set up the ambush was crawling with centipedes, I must have been bitten by one or more of them. I had the same symptoms several months ago when I was on a mission, but they weren't as strong. Centipedes were in our night location on that mission."

"If I knew that's what bit you I would have extracted you," the Lieutenant said, "Those things are real poisonous."

I didn't respond, but sat there wondering what breed of dog the Lieutenant's mother had been. I didn't like having my word that I was sick doubted, and thought that it took a real son of a bitch to admit it to my face.

7

The Field Hospital at Nha Trang

October 30, 1968

Dear Diary,

We had not been back at our firebase long when we learned we were moving, not to a permanent location, but temporarily, to a smaller firebase somewhere near here. The Brigade had begun its' move north to someplace in Kontum Province, but our move isn't going to be right away. It seems that in a move of questionable logic, the Brigade had relocated the infantry company guarding the firebase, leaving the artillery unprotected. They were therefore rushing our platoon of LRPs to the firebase to guard the perimeter. Our personal goods would remain behind, and we carried only what would fit in our packs.

Our temporary home on the firebase was a sea of dust. To compound the situation the tent to which I was assigned was just opposite the helipads. When helicopters took off and landed the rotors stirred up a dust storm reminiscent of depression era Oklahoma. Our clothes, our possessions, and we, ourselves, were covered with dust. Even though we kept our rifles and ammunition covered by our ponchos, they would have to be thoroughly cleaned after every stand of guard duty. The firebase did have showers, of course, and they were almost constantly in use, but no one had brought along enough changes of clothes to keep up with the comings and goings of the helicopters.

Now I'm not the fastidious sort, I could go a day or so with dirt on my clothes, and even on my hands and face. But, when the dust didn't blot it out, the sun was hot, my scalp would sweat, and then a helicopter would take off or land, and my hair and forehead would become caked with mud.

"Enough!" I said after one of these cycles, "If there's a barber on this firebase I'm going to have him shave my head."

Torres, who was lying on his bunk, propped himself up on one elbow. "Hey man," he said, "I know a fellow who has some hair clippers that I could borrow."

"Do you know how to cut hair?" Murphy asked from his bunk.

"Oh, sure man, it's no big deal."

"Ok," I said, "if you can get the clippers you can cut my hair."

At the bigger firebases indigenous Vietnamese would serve as barbers. I guess this base was too small. We are not talking of electric shears, these were the old fashioned hand clippers. The blades look similar to shears you would see in a modern barber shop, but the handles were more like a pair of scissors.

It is important for a LRP to trust the guys in his outfit, you never know when you will have to depend on them in a fight. Torres was my friend, I trusted him. It didn't matter that he had shot at me once, we were friends. Besides, he told me he knew how to use those clippers. Torres lied.

He felt that it was necessary to get a bit or wrist action into his clipping technique. Each time he closed the handles he would bend his wrists thereby lifting the closed blades and tearing out tufts of hair by their roots. Each clip was accompanied by a yelp from me, and peals of laughter from Murphy and Neugard who had gathered to watch my shearing.

Once you start a hair cut you can't stop, especially when you're having it cut to the nubbins. You just can't leave part of it shorn and part of it long.

"Just close your fingers and don't bend your wrist," I kept telling him.

"All right, man, I do it that way," he kept telling me, but he never got the technique exactly right. When he finished a good portion of the hair on the floor included pieces of scalp.

Sheering off my hair seemed like a good idea at the time, but it didn't stop the sun from shining, and it didn't stop the sweat, and it didn't stop the helicopters from coming and going, or the dust from being stirred up. Though my head was easier to clean, some dirt still got into the tiny wounds on my scalp, and the wounds became infected. There was no recourse but sick call.

Some antibiotic salve was all it took to handle the problem of my near scalping by Torres, but while I was there I decided to have the Doctor check out another problem I was having. With all the dirt, I had also developed a boil on my left cheek. No one had noticed the boil because it was the left cheek normally covered by my pants. Upon inspection the Doctor told me that I should have sought treatment sooner, the boil had abscessed.

As we both agreed that I didn't need another orifice in that vicinity, he packed it with antibiotic wadding and told me to return the next day to see how I was progressing. When neither the next day nor the day after my condition showed any improvement the Doctor decided to send me to Nha Trang to recuperate.

Nha Trang is a beautiful little city set on the South China Sea. At least that's what I've been told; all I got to see was the Army field hospital there. Most of the patients were Vietnamese with combat wounds, to my knowledge I was the only one there with my particular malady.

I spent my time lying on my stomach reading books, a routine broken a couple of times a day when I would have to sit it a near scalding sits-bath for a half hour or so.

Now, something should be said about modesty. If you were an American male in Vietnam, and you were modest, it was something of which you would be cured. As the showers were the only plentiful water source, consequently the sits-bath was located in the latrine. And, because of that ready supply of hot water, it was also the place that the Vietnamese mamma-san chose to do the laundry for the hospital staff and cadre. You could be taking a shower, you could be at the urinal, or you could be sitting buck ass naked in a sits-bath, when in walks mamma-san with a basket of laundry. Totally ignoring your presence, she would squat down, her feet flat on the floor, her posterior no more than an inch from the wet surface, and her knee caps even with her head and shoulders, and wash the contents of her basket in the spray from the shower.

The only people in the whole country who seemed to maintain their modesty were Vietnamese men. Whether or not there were women present, and as far as I know even when they were alone, they bathed wearing swimming trunks. It is one of those things that is really none of my business, and I don't wish to in any way besmirch the male population of an entire nation, but I have no evidence that any Vietnamese male past the age of puberty ever washed his genitals.

Within a few days my condition improved, and I was able to move around the ward. Afternoons usually found me sitting, admittedly somewhat delicately, on my right cheek, at the nurses station flirting with the pretty nurse on duty there.

It was on one of these afternoons shortly before my release that a Doctor came rushing in. He was an Army Major that I had never seen before, but he was shaking his head, and ruddy with anger. In November 1968 the movie <u>MASH</u> had not been released and the TV show not even thought of, but as I look back I realize that this Doctor was the living personification of the character, Major Burns.

"Why do people keep calling this a sick ward," the Doctor said, displaying the aura of pomposity which I later related to the <u>MASH</u> character. "The people here aren't sick; they have been honorably wounded in combat with the enemy!"

There was a moment of heavy silence as he looked both to the nurse and to me for a reaction. I looked back at him with great seriousness.

"Then, I shan't mention the nature of my affliction," I said.

The nurse nearly fell out of her chair laughing, and the Doctor just looked bewildered.

8

Back to Bam Me Thuot

Friday November 22, 1968

Dear Diary,

Just out of hospital and I'm back in Bam Me Thuot, but Bam Me Thuot is no longer home for the Second Brigade LRPs. The Platoon, along with most of the rest of the brigade, had moved north to a place called Kontum. Only a few stragglers (like me) are left behind. We are going to make up one final convoy headed north at some indefinite time in the near future. Among the stragglers is one other LRP, a fellow named Bates …

All the tents were gone but one. My foot locker and cot were stored in that tent. The padlock on the footlocker was broken. I opened the lid and inspected the contents. Everything was there that should be except for the pistol I had so recently purchased, and never gotten a chance to fire, and my steel plated Bible. I was disappointed, but I really wasn't angry. War isn't civilized and neither are many of the people who fight in one.

I wasn't angry. Oddly enough, I wished the thief well. I hoped that he would find his booty useful. I hoped that he might find ammunition for the pistol, and have it available if he ever needed it, and I hoped he would find the Bible useful as well. Even though the admonition "Thou shalt not steal" was in the Old Testament rather than the New, there was still plenty there to make him feel guilty. I wasn't angry; I hoped that the steel plate would be as useful to the thief as the text. I hoped that it might save his life from a Vietcong bullet. But, I also hoped that that Vietcong bullet would be at least equal in force to the kick of a mule, and leave the thieving bastard with a bruise in the shape of a Bible.

Bates had set up in a bunker, and I gathered my gear together and moved in with him. There wasn't much for us to do so time drug by. The brigade that took over the firebase fed us. In fact they treated us to a Thanksgiving dinner of lobster, corn on the cob, and boiled potatoes. There were, however, things that only your own brigade could provide. I was in imminent danger of running out of cigarettes, and Bates had this unsatiated desire for C-Ration spaghetti and meatballs. There was only one thing to do, requisition them from those that had them. I speak of course of a midnight requisition.

You must understand that the military has a time honored tradition of finding innovative ways of cutting the red tape in the supply chain. The scrounger is a highly respected member of any unit. I am sure that we could have put in a formal requisition for cigarettes and spaghetti and meatballs, filling out the proper forms, in triplicate of course, and submitting them through channels, and in a few weeks we would have gotten what we wanted, maybe. The American way, however, was to steal them. After all, it all belonged to the Army, and so did we. It wasn't as if you were stealing from a person. It also had the advantage of being more fun than filling out forms in triplicate.

Our target was no more than fifty yards from our bunker, a supply tent just bulging with cases of C-Rations and SP Packs. As is so much in military life, a SP Pack was a redundancy. SP stood for sundry pack, so to call it a SP Pack, or a sundry pack pack, was repetitious, and unnecessary. Inside each of these large cardboard boxes were cigarettes, and soap and jungle chocolate bars (candy bars that were specially designed not to melt in hot humid climate) and all sorts of other stuff, enough to supply a platoon for a month.

Our plan of attack was simple, a head on diversion while the real attack came from the rear. Having assumed command of the operation I assigned to myself the responsibility for the diversion. We waited until after dark when the lights in the tent were out, and the only inhabitant was the supply Sergeant that slept there. I approached the entrance to the tent, gradually beginning to stagger and weave as I got into character.

"Shay," I said throwing open the door to the tent and entering, "ishn't this the plasch where they're hafving a party." I managed to sway as I spoke and slurred my words in my best imitation of a drunk.

The Sergeant sat up in his bunk and clicked on a flashlight. "You woke me up," he said. "Can't you see there's no party here." He tried to level the flashlight on me, but my weaving denied him a clear view of my face.

"Well, where ish it?" I slurred. "They shaid they were hafving a party to schelebrate shometing or other."

"It ain't here. There's nothing here but me, and all I want to do is to go back to sleep."

"Well, damn it, the guys I wash strinking with shaid there was a party in one uf thesh tents around here."

"Get out of here and let me go back to sleep!"

"Are you shure that you don't know where the party ish?"

"Get out of here before I call the MPs and have your ass thrown in the can!"

"Okay, Okay, I'm goin, but you could at leasht be schivle about it." I turned and staggered out hoping that I had bought enough time for Bates to unzip the corner of the tent and remove an SP Pack and a case or two of C-Rations. When I reached the road that ran between the supply tent and our bunker Bates was coming toward me with two cases of C-Rations in his arms.

"Didn't you get a SP Pack?" I whispered.

"Hell yeah," he said. "This is my third trip." When I got to the bunker I found that he had made off with two SP Packs and four cases of C-Rations.

A day or two later our retinue of LRPs grew by one when a LRP named King returned from Recondo School. The School, which, like the Field Hospital, was located in Nha Trang, was where a LRP could learn some of the finer points of his craft. The curriculum included map reading, radio skills, and first aid. There was also a heavy emphasis on physical conditioning that included a seven mile run with a forty pound sandbag in your pack.

Bob Hope had begun his Christmas tour, bringing with him the most popular entertainers and the sexiest starlets. He never made it to Bam Me Thuot. But the USO had not forgotten us. One day we were told that there was to be a show. We went to the location of the show and found an audience of no more than a dozen GIs. Our entertainer was Georgie Gessel. In 1968 Bob Hope was old—Georgie Gessel was ancient. He was accompanied by two women who, though young when compared to Gessel, were old enough to be the mothers of most of their audience.

Their facilities were reminiscent of an old time medicine show. A small stage, barely big enough to hold the three of them, protruded from what looked like a circus wagon. The wagon served both as a dressing room, and a store room for props. Gessel told ancient jokes, and sang songs that Al Jolson had made popular in the teens and twenties, years before any of us had been born. But he performed his heart out for a dozen GIs in the middle of nowhere, and we loved him for it. We didn't miss Bob Hope, those other poor bastards that saw Hope missed Georgie Gessel.

After a few days we were provided with our means of transportation to the north. We were assigned a duce and a half, that we were to drive as far a Pleiku. From there we would go by chopper to Kontum. This vehicle was not just any truck; it was a sway backed nag among trucks. And like an old horse it was blind in one eye and missing a shoe. Blind, in that the right headlight was broken, and handing from its' housing, and missing a shoe, in that there was no spare tire. On top of this its' engine hissed, and coughed as if it were on its last legs. We were told that we would have to get the headlight, and spare tire before it would pass inspection for the convoy, but not to worry about the engine because it had always made it that far before.

It was clear that we were being invited to perpetrate additional larceny. We began to plot our heist. The tools we needed were, luckily, already in the truck. A rusty screwdriver was in the glove compartment, and a lug wrench was in the bed lying near where the spare tire should be. Parts for duce and a halfs were not all over the place. For the most part they were still on the trucks. During the day these parts stores on the hoof, so to speak, were in use hauling all the things that the Army needed to keep it going. At night they were locked up in the motor pool under guard. We couldn't very well just go walking up to one that was unloading stuff at the mess hall, or the ammo dump, remove the things we needed, and then walk back all the way through the camp carrying a headlight and tire. But, as we drove our old nag around, we found that there was one place where duce and a halfs congregated, and to which we had an excuse to go; the fuel depot.

We would pull our caper in broad daylight, just as cool as Frank and Jessie James. On the day before we were scheduled to leave we pulled up to the fuel depot and took our place in line. There were three trucks in front of us. The drivers had all gotten out of their trucks, and were shooting the breeze while their fuel tanks were being filled.

Bates was driving, and had asked to be the diversion on this occasion. He got out and joined the other drivers. King and I got out on the passenger side, and took to our duties. I had the screwdriver, and was assigned to get the headlight. King had the lug wrench, and was to get us a spare tire. I made my way to the lead truck, the one being filled, and leaning against the front fender checked to see that no one was watching. Four screws held the headlight frame. I applied the screwdriver, and had it off and the headlight removed in no time. When I got back to our truck King was already there.

"A tire was loose in the third truck," he whispered. "I didn't even need the lug wrench."

"All filled," said the guy who had been filling the first truck.

Bates glanced our way to make sure I wasn't still working on it, then bid goodbye to the driver. He got in and drove off totally unaware that he was now short one headlight. Then the second, and then the third truck were in turn filled, and went on their way, the driver of the third truck ignorant that he was short a spare tire. We had our truck filled and headed back to our area to properly fit out our swayback nag with its new equipment.

We took turns driving on the trip north. One would drive, and the other two would sit in back getting rid of our excess booty from the raid on the supply tent. There was a shortage of spaghetti and meat balls, but a lot of the other varieties of C-Ration were unconsumed, and we didn't want any questions asked when we got to Pleiku. King and I both smoked and had split up the cigarettes, and packed them away in our footlockers. Still, there was a lot of excess SP Pack contents to dispose of. Whenever we passed through a village we would toss out C-Ration cans, jungle chocolate bars, shaving cream, and bars of soap to the villagers gathered to greet us.

"At that last village I threw them a can of ham and lima beans, and the guy who caught it saw what it was and threw it back," King said factiously. "They don't like those damn things either."

When it was my turn to take the wheel I was amazed at how well the old swaybacked nag was doing. The convoy only moved at between thirty and forty miles per hour, but it felt good to be driving again. "This is the first time I've driven anything since the day before I left home," I told the guys in the back. "I got stopped for speeding then, but there's no chance of that here."

"Did you get a ticket?" King asked.

"The cop wrote one out, and handed it to me and said I was to appear in court on October 15th. I said I couldn't be there because I was leaving for Vietnam the next day. The cop just took back the ticket, and tore it up."

"If I ever get home I'll have to remember that. If the cop doesn't ask to see your orders you could use that excuse anytime."

We were still chuckling when smoke began to pour out from beneath the swaybacked nags hood. She died on the spot. I hope that it wasn't my driving that killed it. Others would have to give it a decent burial, we rode the rest of the way to Pleiku in the back of another unit's duce and a half.

9

Firebase Mary Lou

Tuesday Dec. 3, 1968

Dear Diary,

Today I arrived at the new home of the Second Brigade. I don't know how long we will be here, but it looks like a pretty good place ...

Firebase Mary Lou in Kontum couldn't have been more different than the firebase at Bam Me Thuot. Beside the fact that this firebase had a name, there was the terrain. The firebase at Bam Me Thuot had been on a broad plain, Mary Lou was on a hill. At Bam Me Thuot the jungles were thin and patchy. The jungles around Kontum were triple canopy, dense layers of foliage struggling to reach minuscule patches of sky. In Bam Me Thout the open plain provided multiple spots where a team could be inserted and extracted. In Kontum, LZs were often no more than small holes in the dense jungle.

The LRP cantonment was on a plateau about a hundred yards from the top of the hill. The headquarters tent was located at the head of the parade ground. The only structure on the right side of the parade ground, as you faced the headquarters tent, was the armory conex. A well trodden path that began midway between the Headquarters Tent, and the Conex led up the hill to the rest of Headquarters Company. The only things of interest to LRPs on top of the hill were the Mess Hall, the laundry and the Brigade Tactical Operations Center, a large reinforced bunker known by its acronym, BTOC.

Five sleeping tents in two rows were on the left of the parade grounds. Three tents were in the first row, and two tents and a bunker were in the second. At the foot of the parade ground were the showers, the water wagon and a large bunker. A sixth sleeping tent and another small bunker were just below the large bunker, and were at a ninety degree angle to the other sleeping tents across a small open area.

The LRP cantonment was a beehive of activity when we arrived. Some of the guys were filling sandbags, and stacking them around the base of the tents, and others were tearing apart pallets and using the lumber to build floors in their tents. A couple of other guys were dragging an old parachute into the large bunker.

When we checked in at the headquarters tent we found Shaner in charge. "Well you guys finally decided to join us," he said grinning. "We've got spots in the back row of tents. If you want a floor you're going to have to build it yourself. When you get settled come on back, and get your mail. It's been stacking up here for a couple of weeks."

I found a spot in the back corner of the last tent on the back row. I dropped my footlocker onto a piece of unfloored dirt and unfolded and assembled my cot. I frankly didn't see why anyone needed a floor. I figured that at the most I would be here for no more than ten more months and, judging from my experience so far, it didn't seem that we stayed very long in one spot. The platoon had only been in Bam Me Thuot for a couple of months before I arrived, so I didn't figure we would be here very long either. At least that's how I rationalized it. The truth is I was a lousy carpenter. I could drive nails all right and even saw a reasonably straight line, but when I built something it never quite came out according to design. A dirt floor was better than embarrassing myself with rotten carpentry.

"Hey, welcome back man." A familiar voice greeted me from behind. I turned to see Murphy standing there. "It seems that you've been gone forever."

"Nearly two weeks," I said.

"Well things have been hectic while you've been gone, with the move and everything. There have been a lot of changes, including me. I'm now a team leader."

"Well congratulations," I said. "Maybe I'll get to go out with you sometime."

"I hope so, I've got Torres on my team, and if you were on it, it would seem like old times."

"I don't know about that," I said with a smile. "It seems that Torres wants to either shoot me, or pull out all of my hair."

"Hey, he was shooting at me too, but I've got to admit, I'm not going to let him close to my head with any clippers."

"A wise decision."

"We did have one event on our last mission though. It wasn't Torres that almost got us killed though, it was me. We were setting up our night location.

We had this river on one side. I had heard these stories about Vietcong sneaking up on a camp and turning around the Claymores so when they attacked you'd end up blowing yourselves up instead of them. So, to be sure that didn't happen I decided to set a booby trap just beyond the Claymores. I had a trip wire and an empty C-ration can. You know, I was going to put a grenade in the can, tie one end of the wire to the top of the grenade, and wrap the other end of the wire around a bush on the other side of the path. I decided that so you wouldn't have to pull the grenade all the way out of the can I should break off part of the handle, leaving just enough to hold in on against the side of the C-ration can.

"Well, I broke off too much of the handle and when I pulled the pin the remains of the handle just popped right out of the can, and I was left holding an armed fragmentation grenade in a can.

"I dropped it, shouted 'Oh shit,!' and we all ran for the river, and dove in. We kept ourselves under water until the thing blew."

"Let me think twice about that offer to run with your team," I said grinning.

"Hey, man," he said, sounding a bit like Torres, "I'm in the first tent In the front row. Come and see me when you get settled."

I went back to the headquarters tent to collect my mail. "You've got a pretty good supply of mail here, Reed," Shaner said handing me a box, and a half dozen letters. "This is going to be a good place for us. We've got a hundred yards of hillside separating us from the clerks, cooks, and brass. We've got a volleyball net to put up on the parade ground and we're even going to have our own bar."

"How did we deserve that?"

"It's not so much deserve. The brass was afraid that the mean old Lerps would be a bad example to the guys up on the hill. They didn't want us coming into their EM Club, and tearing it up. So they said we could use that big bunker at the end of the parade ground as our own bar."

"Well at least we'll have a good place to go in case of rocket attack."

"Not quite," Shaner said. "The engineers inspected it and said that it has too much roof surface to ward off a direct mortar, or rocket hit. So if we ever get hit we'll have to squeeze into the two smaller bunkers."

I glanced through the mail. The letters were all from my mother and the box was from my brother. I was about to leave when Shaner gave me some more news.

"Did you know that Festus has left us for the Division Lerps?"

"No," I said looking up in surprise. "What is that all about?"

"He got mad at Captain Connerville, so he contacted Echo 58th and asked if they needed a man with experience. They grabbed him up in three shakes."

"That's too bad, it's a big loss for us." I said.

"There have been some other changes around here too," he said. "I'm acting Platoon Sergeant."

"What happened to Sgt. Blake?"

"When we first moved up here some of the guys snuck a whore into the camp. Twenty guys gang banged her. Poor girl could barely walk when it was time to go home. Anyway five of them caught the clap. Evidently Blake knew about it and didn't do anything. The brass found out, and Blake has been relieved of his duties."

"What are they going to do with him?"

"Probably send him to a line unit. His time with us was almost up anyway. They tend to rotate Officers and Platoon Sergeants every six months. Sometimes they'll start them in a line company then send them to us for the second half of their tour. Other times they'll send them here first."

"What about the girl?"

"She didn't get too much sympathy. She was a professional. By all accounts she got paid. They just turned her loose and she went back to her village."

"Well it's too bad they didn't give her some penicillin before she left."

"They didn't know she had the clap till a couple of days later, when screams started coming from the urinal. Her boyfriends suddenly found out that there was a burning sensation when they tried to pee."

"Well I hope Blake doesn't get in too much trouble." I started to leave then turned back. "How come only five guys got the clap?"

"The others were just lucky I guess."

Back in my tent I tossed the letters on the cot, and opened the box. Inside there was not one, but six knives. Six identical black blades encased in black leather sheaths. British Commando knives were double edged, and hollow ground. The blades were of high carbon steel that would take an edge like no other knife. They tapered to points of elegant fineness. The hilts, beneath their black finish were of heavy brass. The Knife was totally unbalanced, but remarkably when thrown the heavy hilt made these knives turn much faster than other knives, and drove their blades deep into the target. These were the knives that had gained fame in World War II, and still adorned the Special Forces crest. I reserved two for my own use, the other four would be valuable trade goods. My brother had more than fulfilled my request.

The first time I practiced throwing one of my new knives I was reminded of their downside. The British Commando knife is best thrown by the blade, but the fact that they are double edged and super sharp meant that you couldn't throw one without leaving tiny cuts on your fingers. Another problem is that the super fine point seldom lasts very long. By its nature high carbon steel is brittle. The brittleness coupled with the weight of the knife will cause the last half inch of the point to bend. Any attempt to straighten the bent portion of the blade will cause it to snap off, and you must then file down a new point, which, though slightly blunter than the original, would be substantially stronger. In no time at all I had reacquired my boyhood knack for knife throwing, and was consistently sticking the blade in an envelope tacked onto a light post.

Before long I had rigged up a better target. Using some of the pallet lumber that I had refused to use for a floor, I tacked together a solid board, onto which I had painted a rough bull's eye. Knife throwing soon became a rage among the LRPs, and in this department at least, I was pretty much king of the hill.

It was a few days after my arrival at Marylou, and I had just finished defeating a fellow LRP in one such knife throwing contest when I heard a vaguely familiar voice behind me. "Care to try your luck against a Division Lerp?"

When I turned around I saw a face I hadn't seen since before I had come to the Second Brigade. Williams and I had come into country together at Cam Ranh Bay, and then had both been assigned to the Fourth Division. When we both volunteered for LRPs, I was sent to the Second Brigade LRPs, and he remained in Pleiku with the Echo 58th LRPs.

"Williams, good to see you, man," I said. "What brings you to Kontum?"

"I've got a mission to run in this neck of the woods. They must have scheduled it before you guys took over up here. I've been delayed though, my ATL got sick and I have to wait for a replacement. Now," he said pulling a Marine K-Bar knife from its sheath, "about that knife throwing contest."

The contest was closest to the bull's eye, best of seven. On the first throw I hit the bull and Williams was not a half inch off. The second throws were two misses, but Williams was about an inch closer to the bull than I was. On the third throw Williams hit the bull, and I was just outside. On the fourth throw Williams took a three to one lead. I managed to tie the score on the fifth and sixth throws but I couldn't match Williams bull on the last try. Williams had bested me four to three.

"Congratulations," I said, "this is the first time I've ever been beaten in a knife throwing contest."

"It could have gone either way," he said. "You may get me next time—but I doubt it," he said grinning.

We got reacquainted that afternoon, and in the evening I introduced him to the Bunker Bar. I eased my hurt feelings at having lost at throwing knives by lifting a few bucks off him at the poker table.

The next morning as I was putting away my razor and toothbrush Shaner came into my tent. "Captain Connerville wants to see you in the Headquarters Tent," he said.

"Oh, okay," I said having no idea why he wanted to see me. Most platoons only had one officer, a Lieutenant who was Platoon Leader. LRP platoons usually had two officers, a Platoon Leader who could be either a Lieutenant or a Captain, and an Executive Officer who was a Lieutenant.

I entered the Headquarters Tent, and stood at attention in front of the desk where the Captain sat. You didn't salute officers in Vietnam even in base camp. They worked very hard to ensure that you broke the habit so you wouldn't salute them in the field where they could then be marked as a target by a sniper.

"You sent for me Sir," I said.

"Echo Company 58th Infantry has requested that we provide a team member for one of their teams," he said. "The Team Leader, Sergeant Williams has requested that you be that person. Because of chain of command procedures I can't order you to go, however."

"I guess, that I had better volunteer," I said.

"I was hoping you would say that," the Captain said. "You leave this afternoon. The birds are set for fourteen hundred hours."

"Yes, Sir, I'll draw my equipment."

There is no place on earth more magnificent than the jungles of the Central Highlands of Kontum Province. As you flew over them it in a helicopter you looked down on lush triple canopy forests, intersected with sparkling streams that would occasionally plummet over waterfalls, into pools of translucent blue. It was far more rugged and far more beautiful than the more settled lands around Bam Me Thuot.

Once on the ground you are in a green Eden. Mahogany and other hardwoods tower to the skies, hogging as much sunlight as they can consume. The second and third canopies of smaller trees fight for their place in the sun, and become stronger for their struggle. Still, there is enough sun to filter down to the ground level and feed the saplings, the bamboo and, what the GIs called the 'wait a minute vines.'

Not only was the mission with Williams my first taste of the heart of the Central Highlands, but it was also my first mission with Montagnards on the team. There were two of them, with the names of A-Peck and Dong. Dong didn't need a nickname. His real name was, at least in colloquial English, crude enough to bring a chuckle to any GI. A-Peck, however, had to have his name debased, and was soon known to one and all as Pecker.

Dong was not just your run of the mill Montagnards, he was what we called a "cowboy." Officially he was a Kit Carson Scout, a Vietcong or North Vietnamese that had been captured, and had changed sides to fight for the South and their American allies. It didn't matter that the real Kit Carson was more familiar with trapping beaver than he was with driving cattle, to a GI he was part of the old west and was not an Indian, therefore, he was a cowboy.

The first night when we set out our Claymores Dong took an especially long time. When he came back Williams took me to where he had hidden the Claymore to show me what a fine job he had done. What I saw was the outline of a Claymore mine done in twigs. Granted you couldn't see any of the olive drab color or the words "Front; this side toward Enemy," but still it looked like a folk art rendition of a claymore done in twigs. Before I went back I pulled some grass and carefully laid it over the twigs to break up the outline. I made a mental note that if this was an example of Vietcong camouflage, I should have no trouble recognizing it in the future.

As we settled in for the night Pecker and Dong sat quietly occasionally whispering to each other in their native tongue. The heaviest conversation was between Williams and me.

"I wonder what's happening back in the world," Williams said. To American GIs in Vietnam 'the world' meant the United States.

"Probably more anti-war protests, and political bickering," I said.

"A lot of our generation are protesting the war. Some have even given up their citizenship; they picked up and moved to Canada."

"That's there right if they want," I said. "I don't hold it against anybody who is willing to migrate for their convictions, but I'll be really pissed if, when this thing is over, they want to come back."

"Most of them seem to be hippies, spoiled rich kids that say they're searching for themselves, but really are afraid of getting their asses shot off over here." Williams took a bite of a jungle chocolate bar. "What do you think about this war, Reed?"

"War is nearly always a bad idea, maybe this one is especially. But, I can't go along with those that say that this is an immoral war. It may be the most moral war we ever fought. We don't have anything to gain. Nobody really attacked us, like at Pearl Harbor. If we win, then the South Vietnamese will be free from domination by the north. They may have the freedom to have real democratic elections, to worship God or Buddha, or whoever the hell they want to worship, maybe even to speak and write what they think. But, we won't get anything out of it.

"The hippies have a saying, 'what if they gave a war and no one came.' I like that. But, it can't just be us, it just can't be Americans, it's got to be the people of North Vietnam, the people of China, and the People of Russia too. It has got to be all the people in the world. But, until all those people have the freedom to make such decisions as war and peace for themselves, until their political bosses care what those people think, until then, there will be grunts like us out in the middle of some jungle, wondering how in the hell we got into such a mess." I had expressed my thoughts in a couple of letters home, but this was the first time I expressed my thoughts to another GI.

Behind us the cracking of bamboo told us that we were not alone. Grabbing our rifles we turned and peered into the darkening jungle. About a hundred yards away a large stag brushed the bamboo from around him with his antlers, and settled down to the ground to sleep. Our night location was safe, if he was unaware of our presence the chance of us being found by the North Vietnamese was pretty slim.

The AO was cold. We found no recently traveled trails, no bunker complexes, and no signs of enemy activity. But for me it was a successful mission. It allowed me to familiarize myself with the jungles I would be living in four days a week for the next eight months, to get comfortable with the terrain and the density of the vegetation.

I've always felt at home in the forests, be they jungle or woods. From above, this jungle was vast and impenetrable, but once you were on the ground, and saw it in microcosm, the jungles of the Central Highlands of Vietnam didn't feel greatly different than the woods of the Ozark Mountains of Missouri. Some of the animals were the same. The stag didn't look much different than the white tail back home. On the other hand some creatures were completely different. There were no long tail monkeys in the Ozarks, and most of the snakes of Vietnam were much more deadly than the copperheads and water moccasins of Missouri. But, still I felt at home. I had known since my youth how to walk without rustling leaves, or breaking twigs. My eyes were accustomed to the forms made of sunlight and shade dancing through dense foliage, my ears were attuned to the singing of birds, even though they were not always the same birds, and to the skittering of small animals. When we returned to Mary Lou I felt myself a more seasoned LRP.

10

Conflict Between Brothers

Sunday December 6, 1968

Dear Diary,

I don't know where I got the idea, but it seemed logical, LRPs shouldn't fight each other. When we were out there, on a mission, we had to operate like a well oiled machine. The odds were we were going to be outnumbered, if we didn't care whether a member of our team lived or died, well when that happened it weakened the whole team …

It was late on the first night after my return from the field. I had had a few drinks with some of the guys in the Bunker Bar, but nobody had been interested in playing poker so I went back to my tent to read. Among the books that some good hearted people in the States had sent to Vietnam, and that had found their way to Firebase Mary Lou, I found a copy of a book by Will and Ariel Durant's called <u>Rousseau and Revolution.</u> As I was the only history buff in the outfit, I grabbed it. It was a large tome, too big to take to the field, Agatha Christy, and Erle Stanley Garner paperbacks were better for that, but I could get more deeply involved when I was in base camp, and this epoch of the French Revolution provided hours of distraction.

It was late, after 22 hundred hours, and the camp was still noisy. Nearly all of the tents still had lights, on and the constant hum of indistinct voices seemed to rise to a new crescendo. I looked up from my book, and concentrated on the sound, but was far enough away that I couldn't make out the words. Then I heard someone rushing down the lane between the rows of tents. The tent flap was pushed back and Torres burst in.

"Hey, man," he said, the anxiety showing in his voice, "some guys are trying to pick a fight with Murphy."

"Who are they?" I said sitting up in my bunk.

"I don't know, man. Some guy who just got back from reenlistment leave. All the old guys are on his side."

"I'll be right there." I opened my footlocker and grabbed two of my knives and stuffed them into the back of my belt beneath my jungle fatigue shirt.

The commotion was coming from the last tent in the front row. Torres was waiting for me by the back entrance. As we entered I surveyed the situation. The center of attention was a tall fellow sitting on a bunk in the middle of the tent. Murphy was standing at his side holding a grenade launcher in his right hand. The guy on the bunk was obviously drunk. He weaved slightly in his seat and his voice was slurred.

"You cock sucking bastard, you haven't got the balls to be a Lerp," he bellowed a Murphy. "I'm going to take your ass and wipe up this fucking tent with it."

Murphy didn't answer. He just stood there.

Other LRPs were seated on bunks around the room, there may have been as many as fifteen or twenty of them. All were facing the duo in the middle. I moved behind the last bunk on the left where three guys were sitting. I hadn't come to fight Murphy's fight for him, but hoped to ensure that it didn't turn into an all out riot. I never liked bullies, or bullying, and on several occasions had through the intimidation of my size caused a bully to back down. But that wasn't going to work here, the bully was at least as large as I was, and had the crowd on his side. I wished that Colbray had been there, but he wasn't. I didn't know what I would do if trouble broke out. I wasn't going to knife anyone, but maybe just having them would give potential assailants second thoughts about coming after me and allow me to try to talk some sense into them. Unfortunately the officers and MPs were on top the hill, a quarter mile away.

"Well, mother fucker, what are you going to do about it," the drunk said as he attempted to get to his feet.

Murphy didn't tell him what he was going to do about it, he did it. He suddenly lashed out with the M-79 smashing the barrel into the fellow's ribs, and knocking him back onto the bunk. Almost instantly another swing came, this time laying the barrel across the guys forehead.

Before anyone could do anything to stop him Murphy turned on his heels and rushed through the front entry to the tent. Nobody took after him, their first reaction was to see if they could help the drunk. The guy was dazed, and bleeding, but still conscious. By the time some of his closest buddies decided to seek revenge, officers appeared and restored order.

All of those who were there had to give written statements, and be interviewed by Captain Connerville. It was after midnight when my turn came. I wrote out what I had seen and brought it to the Captain.

"What were you doing there?" Connerville asked.

"Torres came and got me from my tent. He said that Murphy was in trouble."

"Murphy is your friend?"

"Yes, Sir."

"So, you wanted to fight for your friend?"

"No, Sir, I wanted to stop a fight before one got started. It's stupid for us to fight each other, we have to depend on each other when we're out there, and you can't build trust by picking fights like that guy did." I said.

"Sergeant Boggs?" for the first time I heard the drunk's name.

"Yes, Sir. I didn't know his name, but the guy that got his head broken open."

"You said that Specialist Murphy hit him twice, no one else saw more than one hit."

"I saw two hits, Sir. I can't very well control what others see."

"Why did Boggs, pick the fight?" Connerville asked.

"Pecking order, I guess. I hear he's been gone for a while, I guess he wanted to make sure that everybody sill knew that he was the meanest SOB in the valley." The Captain looked surprised that an enlisted man would try to ascribe psychological motivations to what had happened.

"Yea, though I walk through the valley of death I will fear no evil, for I am the meanest SOB in the valley," he said, quoting in full a common inscription found on Zippo lighters in Vietnam.

"That's the way I figure it," I said. "He didn't know Murphy well enough to hate him that much."

"Well, your friend Murphy is in deep trouble," he said. "He hasn't come in yet, and we may have to send the MPs to find him."

"Is Boggs going to be all right?"

"It looks like it, but he's going to be hurting for a few days."

"Can you hold off a while on calling in the MPs, Sir? I'd like to try to find Murphy, and see if I can persuade him to come and see you."

"I've got five or six more interviews. I won't do anything until after that. That should take a couple of hours."

"Thank you, Sir."

"You're dismissed."

I didn't know where he would be. I had to use instinct, and personal experience to try to find him. Outside the headquarters tent I was faced with my first choices. Would Murphy have gone up the hill toward the heart of the camp, or down the hill toward the perimeter, and the helicopter pads. He was scared and knew he was in trouble, he probably didn't think he had a friend in the world. I chose to go down the hill. A hundred yards or so down the hill the road forked, the right branch going further down the hill to the perimeter, and the left fork bending around a little patch of woods, and climbing up the hill to the rear of the camp. I lit a cigarette, thought a minute.

If he went toward the perimeter, he would be faced with guard towers and guards at the main gate. He couldn't get off the firebase without going through the gate or across a mine field. I turned left.

The woods were thin, after all they were in the middle of a firebase, GIs cut through them on a regular basis taking short cuts from one road to another, but near the middle of the woods was one patch of heavy brush. I had moved far from the lights of the LRP area, and my eyes had become accustomed to the darkness. I stomped out my cigarette and moved toward the bush. Behind it, leaning against a tree that was too small to hide him was a shadowy figure.

"You want to talk, Murph?" I said.

"Is that you, Reed," he said.

"Yeah, it's me," I said moving to his side of the bush and squatting down. He did the same.

"How'd you know it was me?"

"There aren't too many guys hiding out right now."

"I'm in deep trouble."

"Yeah, I guess you are."

"I didn't want to fight that guy, but he wouldn't let up."

"It didn't turn out to be much of a fight."

"If I'd let him get up he would have killed me."

"Nah, he would have just wiped up the tent with your ass."

Murphy gave a little nervous laugh. "How bad is he?"

"He'll have a bandage around his head, and a nasty headache for a few days, but he'll live."

"I'm in deep shit," he said.

"Yeah," I said, "but hiding isn't going to do you any good. Before long they'll have MPs with flashlights looking for you. I found you, so will they."

"How did you know where I'd be?"

"You're a Lerp, you'd find the first patch of brush you could to hide behind. Besides, I've had some experience running away and hiding."

"You?—When?"

"When I was at Fort Benning, in Officers Candidate School. I'd taken all the harassment I could from the training officers. I decided that the only way they would kick me out was if I went AWOL. So I took off. I hid out until about noon the next day, and then went back thinking they would kick me out. They said I hadn't been gone long enough, you had to be gone twenty-four hours before you were officially AWOL, and they were going to give me twice as much shit to make up for it."

"It's not the same thing. You ran off to try to get into trouble, and I ran off to try to get away from trouble."

"It didn't work for either of us, Murph. Especially not for you. You've got no place to go. An AWOL American is going to be easy to find in any town or village in Vietnam. You can't continue to hide on the firebase, it's not that big."

"What can I do?"

"The Captain is still interviewing everybody who was there," I said. "Don't you think he should hear your side of the story?"

"But the guys are all against me."

"I told the story straight, some of them probable will too. Nobody's going to break into the headquarters tent, and take you away from the Captain just to beat you up."

"Okay," he said. "I guess you're right."

"Let's go," I said.

We walked together in silence as far as the parade ground. "Good luck," I said taking his hand and shaking it firmly. I watched as he crossed the last few yards alone. His head was down, and his shoulders drooped. He was a far cry from the proud, and excited LRP that had greeted me when I arrived at Marylou. He stopped at the entry to the tent, and looked back at me, then he straightened up, raised his head, and entered the tent.

I didn't know it then, but that was the last time I saw Murphy. Both Boggs and he were drummed out of the unit. The next day Murphy was shipped back to Echo Company and from there was reassigned to another unit. I lost track of him, and it would be three months before I would hear of him again.

11

Contact?

Sunday December 8, 1968

Dear Diary,

The Central Highlands is honey combed with rivers, rivers that run through broad, deep valleys, and are joined by tributary rivulets, and creeks bringing more valleys into the network. One of these networks is the Plei Trap Valley. The Plei Trap Valley meanders southeast from where the border between Laos and Cambodia touch the western border of Vietnam, and from there thrusts deep into the heart of the Central Highlands.

It is a principle artery of that route of covert entry and egress that has come to be known as the Ho Chi Min trail. When we moved to Kontum the Second Brigade LRPs earned the responsibility of patrolling the Plei Trap Valley, of monitoring the myriad of trails that brings troops and supplies from North Vietnam, through Laos and Cambodia, and into South Vietnam's Central Highlands.

Two days after I watched Murphy walk away for that last time, my name appeared on the board in the HQ. I was to go out the next morning with Adams as Team Leader and a guy named Tyler as ATL. The forth man was a Montagnard named Dok.

Dok was short and wiry. But that description could match almost all of the Montagnards. Where Doc differed from most the others is that looked younger. He wasn't he just looked that way. He didn't look as weathered as the rest. But like most of the others he was a good addition to the team. He was tough as nails and knew how to move in the jungle, to walk quietly and to be aware of everything around him. This was going to be important because we were going into the Plei Trap.

We arrived in our AO on schedule. Adams was carrying his sawed-off M-14 and Tyler had a CAR-15. Dok and I carried M-16s, and I also carried the M-79. The AO was only a couple of kilometers from the border. We were inserted on high ground, and after lying dog for about a half hour moved south along a ridge. To the east the ridge fell off quite precipitously into a broad open valley. The floor of the valley was pockmarked with bomb craters.

For a while we followed a well beaten path that crossed the ridge. Near where the path started its decent down the hill we came across the largest pile of dung any of us had ever seen.

"Elephant?" I asked in a LRP whisper.

"Either that or the biggest damn water buffalo that ever was," Tyler said.

We looked at Dok. He just shrugged. "Too big water buffalo," he said.

Adams led us off the trail, and along the edge of the ridge. We could see where the trail cut diagonally across the hill and exited the jungle into the open valley. After paralleling the trail for about a hundred yards we stopped to eat lunch.

We had heated some water and poured it over our rations, Adams folded the top of his ration bag and stuck it in the leg pocket of his camouflaged fatigues.

"Reed, you and Dok stay here and guard the back door. Tyler and I are going down the hill, and set up where we can watch the trail."

Tyler wrapped up his LRP ration, grabbed his CAR-15, and followed Adams down the hill. Dok and I set out Claymores, his aimed down the ridge and mine back toward where we had come. I didn't like the idea of splitting up a four man team. If attacked Dok and I weren't close enough to support them, and they weren't close enough to support us if we were hit.

But Adams was team leader, and had a lot more experience than I did. But, still something just didn't feel right. I couldn't put my finger on it, but I was uncomfortable. I finished my meal, dug a hole with my commando knife, and buried the trash, then lit a cigarette, and as instructed, kept watch in the direction that we came from. Dok in complete silence was watching the ridge in the opposite direction.

It was quiet and peaceful. The top ridge was more like a wooded park than a jungle. The canopy of towering mahoganies was thick enough to stunt the growth of underbrush. The trees were spaced at five or six yard intervals. The undergrowth did not begin until the hill sloped downward toward the valley. We could hear the twittering of birds, high up in the canopy above our heads. Thirty or forty minutes passed in silence.

This tranquility was broken by the sudden burst of automatic weapons fire. Both Dok and I tensely pulled our weapons close across our bodies, and swung around to face the direction of the gunfire.

Adams and Tyler burst through the undergrowth, and onto the ridge, at a full run. "We ambushed some NVA down there," Adams yelled. "We've got to get out of here."

Dok and I blew our Claymores rather than take the time to gather them up. We jumped to our feet and started off. "Your pack," Tyler shouted.

"There's nothing I need in there," I replied. I had decided early in my tour, perhaps after lugging Colbray's massive pack, that if I had to run for it I wasn't going to be burdened by a pack if it didn't have a radio or Claymore in it. I carried all my ammunition, grenades and a full canteen on my web belt. A LRP Ration, and spare cigarettes were in the leg pockets of my camouflage fatigues. The enemy could capture my bedroll, and my other canteens and rations, they would be less likely to capture me if I left them behind.

Our retreat found me in the unusual position of being point instead of rear security. I found a narrow trail down the other side of the ridge and led the team down it.

"Go, go!" Adams was shouting behind me.

The path was narrow and I had to push the brush on my right aside with my M-16 and on the left with my free hand. I was moving as fast as I could in those conditions. Then with the crack of a rifle, and the spurt of dust from a bullet ricocheting off the ground between my feet, I found I could move faster.

At the bottom of the ridge was a small creek and then the terrain rose quickly again to another ridge.

"Look there," Adams said pointing to a bomb crater mid way up the second ridge. "We can hole up there, and call in some gun ships."

The jungle around a bomb crater is always difficult to navigate. Downed trees form a natural abatis, and bamboo stalks seem to weave together to impede your passage. But we fought our way through, and hurled ourselves against the dirt face of the crater. I reached up to make sure the safety was off my rifle. It was off, but I switched it from semiautomatic to full automatic. As I did I noticed that the dust cover that protected the bolt was open. As I hadn't fired the rifle, it must have been popped open as I pushed brush aside along the trail.

"You should have seen those guys," Tyler was saying as Adams called in the contact. "Some of them were the biggest Vietnamese I've ever seen. More than six foot tall, there just aren't any Vietnamese that tall. I don't think they were Vietnamese at all, I think they were Chinese advisers, or maybe even Russians. I've heard rumors of Chinese and Russian advisors that end up doing the fighting. I think we just ran into them."

Nothing was moving across the valley. There was no shooting, no shouting of orders in a foreign tongue, all was quiet. Still we stayed alert watching for any sign of the enemy, and Tyler kept babbling, now in a LRP whisper, about the number and size of the unit that they had hit.

Adams slipped the handset through the loop on his web suspenders. "There's a FAC plane in the area that's coming in to try to draw their fire," he said changing the magazine in his sawed off M-14. A FAC was a Forward Air Controller, an Airforce Pilot that flew a small lightly armed plane scouting for targets for aircraft.

Before long we heard the drone of his engines, then in a few more seconds, we saw a small twin tailed aircraft with rocket pods under its wings. The rockets were considered as smoke rockets, but as they also contained white phosphorus, they had a bite to them. Adams raised the pilot on the radio, and Tyler used his signal mirror to help the pilot locate our position.

"Roger Star Shiner six three," I heard Adams say into the handset, "That's our location. Have you seen anything of the bad guys?"

He listened to the FAC's response and we watched as the plain flew low, and slow, back and forth, across the hills. "Roger," Adams finally said, "that would be near where we hit them. Thanks and out."

He lowered the handset. "He said that he got some ground fire a couple of klicks north of here, but nothing on this side of the ridge."

"Well lets get some choppers in here and get out of here," Tyler said.

"Good idea," Adams said and once again brought the handset to his ear and mouth. "Seven-Niner Charlie, this is Two Bravo over." A couple of seconds later, "Roger Seven-Niner Charlie, we need extraction, are the birds on their way?" A long pause, then, "roger out."

He hung the handset back on his web suspenders. "They want us to walk out," he said. "Something's going on that has all the choppers tied up. He says there is a Special Forces encampment four or five klicks south of here where we can get a ride back to Mary Lou."

Adams located our destination on his map, took a compass reading and we headed out. Once again I took up my place as rear security. Dok and I tried to maintain a discipline in our movements but Adams and Tyler acted as if they were just out for a walk. They made no effort to walk quietly, and carried their weapons by their side. I don't know if they thought it was safe because the enemy was behind us, or if they were just sloppy. Just because one set of enemies was behind us, it didn't mean that others couldn't be in front. About a kilometer after we started we reached a well traveled gravel road. It evidently led to our destination so we took it. If following trails in the jungle was dangerous then following a road had to be idiocy.

My earlier discomfort had abated in the excitement of the escape, but now it returned in spades. Even though I tried to concentrate on my duties as rear security, and added to it the need to watch the tree lines on either side, the easy walking on the road gave me time to think. I didn't like what I was thinking.

I'd heard stories about false contacts. About LRPs who tried to build their own image, or just to get out of the jungle quicker, by faking contact with the enemy, and then calling for an early extraction. Had I been duped into supporting a false contact dreamed up by Adams and Tyler? They were the only ones that had seen the enemy. They had split the team up making it impossible for Dok and I to lend support. I had heard firing, but I didn't know if all of it came from their weapons or if some had come from the bad guys.

I thought about the bullet that had whizzed between my legs. I had heard that shot, and it seemed close. But why hadn't they fired again? Then I remembered the dust cover of my M-16 being open. Maybe the brush hadn't caused it to pop open. A shot would have opened it, it was designed to open with the first shot. Had I accidentally fired my rifle? I hadn't felt the recoil of a shot, and an M-16 had enough recoil that I should have felt it, and the noise of the shot didn't seem that close. But, my adrenaline had been pumping so maybe I wouldn't have felt the kick of the rifle, and maybe it would have muffled the noise of the report, too. Still, the dust spout had been in front of me and the dirt had sprayed forward indicating a bullet trajectory that didn't seem possible from my weapon.

The Forward Air Controller had gotten ground fire, but I hadn't heard him say so, I only had Adams word for it. Even if the FAC had reported it, it could have been reflections from objects on the ground, or even his own imagination. Sometimes we see things because we expect to see them. This was the third time that I may have been in contact with the enemy, but I had never seen the enemy. I couldn't be sure of any of them.

Ray Barrio and Ed Mateer

LRPs say goodbye to fallen brothers

LRP hats stand in for fallen LRPs

Sgt. Larry Massoletti

Picture from the pack of enemy soldier

Sgt Clyde Hinkle

Camp Mary Lou

Tom Reed

Massoletti on Mission

Ronald Neugard

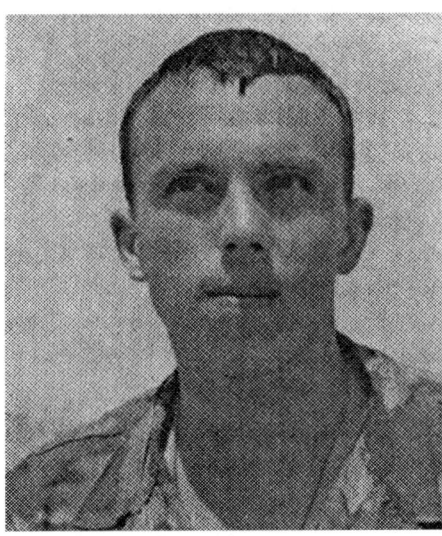

Robert Plaskett

12

The Holidays 1968

Saturday December 14, 1968

Dear Diary,

I am now entering my third month as a LRP. My appearance has changed since that October day that I arrived I in Bam Me Thuot. My upper lip now sports a moustache that droops to the corners of my lips, the maximum length that the army allows. I now shun olive drab jungle fatigues in favor of camouflaged fatigues called trees. The only olive drab I wore was my Second Brigade LRP hat.

I have also managed to obtain a replacement for the stolen Ruger pistol. I paid an exorbitant $300 for a 38 caliber double-derringer that would have cost no more than $125 in the States. But I'm not in the States and handguns, any handguns, sell for a premium over here.

What else was I going to spend my money on? The army didn't pay you much. I think my paycheck came to about $110 a month, and that included hazardous duty pay for being in Vietnam. But at the same time there wasn't a lot to spend your money on. There were the prostitutes, but they were cheap. The best of the lot didn't cost you more than twenty bucks, and you had to get off base to spend that. That didn't happen that often. Booze was cheap. The Bunker Bar was pretty much of a non-profit operation. Beer was a quarter and hard liquor was fifth cents a shot. We just tried to make enough to replace the booze we drank. Then there were the poker games. But I wasn't spending money there either. In fact I was showing a healthy profit from my gambling. So the fact was I had money to burn, and an overpriced pistol seemed to be just the way to spend it.

Luckily 38 Special ammunition was easier to obtain than 22, the airforce still issued 38s to pilots. The little gun came with a shoulder holster that made it easy to hide beneath my trees.

The ornaments on my collars had also changed. Now, on those rare occasions when I chose to wear my rank, instead of the inverted chevron and rocker of a PFC, I wore the insignia of a Specialist Forth Class. When the Headquarters Company Commander handed me the orders for my promotion he seemed disappointed that I wasn't more excited about it. I knew that I was being promoted not for any meritorious action on my part, but because some calendar said it was time for me to be promoted, and I hadn't fouled up badly enough to prevent it. It did mean a little more money paid into my account each month, but as I said, I already was having trouble spending what they gave me and it wouldn't add or detract one whit to or from the respect I got from fellow LRPs. Officers, to whom rank meant so much, didn't seem to understand that rank didn't mean much among the rank and file LRPs.

In some ways I've always lived in my own unrealistic and very idealistic world. In that world, merit and ability are rewarded because they lead to the success of the mission. In that world, leaders see the transparency of ambitious sycophants. In my ideal world, a leader makes decisions objectively, based on facts, not emotionally, based on their personal likes or dislikes. In that world, a Harvard or Oxford education may be no more valid than one from Central Missouri State, or, for that matter, no more valid than the life experience of a self educated person. For me these were tenets of faith, accepted without regard to any evidence seen before, or since. Needles to say, I have often been disappointed in the actions of "bosses" in the real world.

Life in the LRP cantonment between missions was falling into a routine. Usually, if you were just back from a mission they wouldn't bother you with details, or guard duty. Other than policing up cigarette butts in the morning, the day was pretty much yours to do what you wanted. For me that usually entailed reading and writing letters home. They had erected a volleyball net on the parade ground, and if you wanted some exercise there was usually a game going on, and somebody on one team or the other that wanted to be spelled for a game or two.

At night we had the Bunker Bar, stocked with booze and beer purchased from the Green Beret. There was almost always a poker game going on, or if you preferred you could just sit and visit, and down a few beers, or your cocktail of choice, provided it wasn't too exotic. The bar was **usually** pretty well stocked. Though we might not have your favorite brands, we were guaranteed to have something you could palate. We had two or three brands of bourbon, a couple of

Scotches, gin, vodka and Cognac on the shelf, and plenty of beer and soda pops in the cooler under the bar. For most guys choosing a mixed drink wasn't a problem, so long as it was bourbon, scotch, gin, vodka, or even Cognac mixed with Coke or Seven-up.

Usually I just drank my bourbon with ice only, but occasionally I wanted something different. A dry martini sounded good, but to my knowledge there wasn't a bottle of dry vermouth anywhere in the Central Highlands. So, if you couldn't find a bottle of cheap Italian wine, why not substitute an expensive distilled French wine? A few drops of Cognac sprinkled into the gin and shaken (not stirred) in a plastic canteen that had ice cubes forced down its throat, and voila, the Hardship Tour Martini was born. I named it with my tongue deeply imbedded in my cheek. The Army considered service in Vietnam to be a "hardship tour." It seemed that only in the American Army, where GIs got Care packages filled with Hostess Twinkies, and where Lobster was served for Thanksgiving Dinner, would you make a martini substituting four star Cognac for cheap vermouth.

There were those among us who preferred to inhale their intoxicants. There was no doubt about it. A lot of dope was smoked in Vietnam. Some nights I felt I could float to my bunk on the clouds of smoke in my tent. We didn't worry about the MPs they came down to the LRP cantonment to smoke with out guys. Some guys seemed to compete with each other to see who the biggest pot head was.

The form of marijuana prevalent in Vietnam was called Montagnard Magic. I have been told that it was a most excellent weed, though I personally avoided indulging in it during my tour of duty. I had no moral objection to smoking pot, and I didn't believed the anti drug propaganda that preached that the use of marijuana would automatically cause you to move on to more addictive drugs. I didn't smoke it because I could see myself, in the midst of some mortar or rocket attack, sitting on top of the Bunker Bar, lighting up another joint, and watched all the pretty fireworks.

For better or worse, I could hold my booze. I drank to be social, and because I liked the taste of liquor, not to get drunk. The only reason for smoking marijuana was to get high, and, to me at least, that didn't seem such a good idea in the middle of a combat zone.

It was around the middle of the month that Captain Connerville became Company Commander of Headquarters Company, and was replaced as LRP Platoon Leader by a Lieutenant named Miller. There were other changes as well. Of the ten FNGs that had come into the platoon in October, only three were left, Torres, Neugard and me.

It was around this time too, that I ran a mission with Jerry Hancock. We got to know each other huddled against the ground on a ridge, watching through a break in the foliage, as a Forward Air Controller directed Air Force jets against an enemy that was in our Area of Operations. The FAC knew we were there, and contacted Hancock to let us know what was going on. We clearly saw the jets making their passes over a jungle target less than a kilometer away. We saw the release of the bombs, heard the loud explosion, and felt the earth quake beneath us in response to their assault.

In a quieter time on that mission Jerry took some of his poems from his pack, and let me read them. On that mission Jerry Hancock and I formed a bond of friendship.

We never ran another mission together. Shortly after we returned to Mary Lou, Jerry left to meet his wife in Hawaii, where she joined him on his R and R. I went on missions with other Team Leaders. But, when ever we were both in base camp we would drift into the Bunker Bar, and spend hours just drinking and talking. I probably knew more about Jerry Hancock, and he knew more about me, that did anyone outside of our own families.

"When I was In College I probably played as much Bridge as Poker," I told him one day as we sipped on a couple of beers. "My girl friend Karen had a friend who was married. We would go over to their apartment to play. They're the ones that taught me the game."

"I didn't know you played bridge," Jerry said. "Looks like we've got that in common too. Are you any good?"

"If I take the time to count trump, and plan my play I do okay, but I have a bad habit of playing by the seat of my pants, and that can get me in trouble."

"It will do it every time," he said. "You know it's strange you mention bridge, I was talking to Lieutenant Miller the other day and he asked me if I knew anybody that played bridge. He's been trying to get up a game. He said one of the officers from BTOC played. If you want we might be able to arrange a game, us against them."

"Sounds like fun, but I hate to take on a couple of officers and not beat them."

"Then remember to count your trumps, and plan your Play."

So an occasional night of bridge was added to my diversions at Mary Lou. The officers played on our turf, the Bunker Bar. Unfortunately my skills were not such that I often came out a winner. I didn't think I would enjoy losing to officers, but my disdain for them was softened by the friendliness, and good company.

We did play for money, but the half cent a point wager did not dig deeply into my wallet, and I was usually able to off-set my losses by getting into a poker game once the officers left. I was never able to talk the officers into staying around for a poker game. If the officers played poker it was with other officers, and the game was off limits to enlisted men.

A few days before Christmas my care package arrived from home. My Mother had asked what I needed in one of her letters, and I immediately thought of means of supplementing my diet in the field. I asked for bags of peanuts and beef jerky. As an after thought, I mentioned that when I was home I had occasionally enjoyed a Gold Label Romano cigar, and asked that she send me a box. Maybe I just didn't understand mothers. Or maybe it was just that my mother never did anything half way. When the Care package arrived there were twelve cartons of bagged peanuts, three boxes of individually wrapped beef jerky and there were two boxes of the cigars I liked.

Bags of peanuts and sticks of beef jerky would accompany me on my missions for the next three months with enough left to be shared with friends in the platoon. The cigars were another story. Though I did enjoy them, I enjoyed them at a rate of one or two a day when I was in base camp. Cigars were too smelly to be smoked in the field, so those forty cigars should have lasted through most of my tour of duty. Whether my mother hoped to replace my cigarette habit, or just didn't understand that I couldn't smoke that many cigars, another two boxes arrived two weeks later and they kept coming every two weeks until I finally wrote home, and informed her that I had sufficient cigars to supply every cigar smoker in the Forth Division for the next year.

The war didn't slow down for Christmas. As was usual, at any given time half the platoon was in the field. I was lucky enough to be in the half that was in base camp for Christmas. Not that there was a great deal of celebrating, but anytime you were in base camp there was a greatly reduced likelihood of being shot at, which in itself was a reason for celebration. Some of the guys put decorations around the Bunker Bar, but it was awful hard to get into the Christmas spirit when your family is half a world away.

On Christmas Eve night I took a turn behind the bar. It gave me an opportunity to come up with a new drink to try to make the night a bit more festive. I gave the first example to Neugard.

"What is it?" he asked.

"I call it a Hardship Tour Purple Passion," I told him.

"What's it got in it?"

"A shot of vodka, a shot of Cognac, and it's topped off with Grape Nehi."

He took another sip. "It tastes just like Grape Nehi," he said.

"Then it could be a success. It seems that the only reason these guys want a mixer is to kill the taste of the booze."

"Yeah," he said, pushing the drink back toward me. "Give me a beer."

Mundy came in carrying a PRC-25. He was a short timer that had been with the LRPs for the better part of two tours. He was finishing out his second tour as Supply Sergeant.

"We've got a team in contact," he said. "I thought you guys would want to listen in." He attached the long antenna and switched on the radio. "Give me a beer," he said shoving some scrip across the bar.

"Who is it?" I asked handing him a beer.

"Taylor and Mele," Mundy said.

"Seven-Niner Charlie," the radio crackled with Taylors' voice, "what is the ETA on those birds? Over!"

"Hang in there two Bravo." the Seven Niner Charlie said. "They should be there within fifteen or twenty minutes. Have you located a LZ? Over."

"We're headed for the blue line we crossed earlier today. We should reach it pretty quick now. Over!"

"A night, river extraction," Mundy said looking at Shaner who had come in during the exchange between Reynolds and Seven Niner Charlie. "That sounds too much like the Finley fiasco."

"We've got a different group of pilots now," Shaner said. "Those Bikini pilots are pretty damn good."

"Didn't we have a contact last Christmas too?" Mundy asked.

Shaner thought a minute. "Yeah, we sure did. That was back at the Oasis. The Team Leader and Assistant Team Leader about peed in their pants they were so scared ..."

The radio interrupted Shaner's story.

"We're at the blue line now," Taylor said. "How much longer for the birds? Over."

"They're no more than ten minutes from your location," Seven Niner Charlie reported. "They should be contacting you shortly. Over."

"Roger, they had better get here quick. The bad guys aren't that far behind us. Over."

"Hang in there, Two Bravo. Over." The radio once again lapsed into silence.

"In last year's contact, as I remember it," Shaner took up his story again, "Jarvis was walking rear security, and heard voices behind them. He's the one that told me the story. He said that they puled off the trail in the middle of some waitaminute vines, and set up to wait for the bad guys."

"Didn't they have a Yard with them on that mission?"

"No, it was a South Vietnamese guy, from the ARVN Special Forces. He went out with some of our teams to learn our tactics. Anyway, the bad guys had just come even with them when a helicopter flies over and the bad guys take cover in the waitaminutes too. They're no more than a couple of feet in front of our guys. Jarvis motioned to the Team Leader, or ATL, I don't remember which, that he was going to use his knife on one, and he should do the same to the other. But, the Team Leader waves him off, and as soon as the chopper passed the bad guys moved on not knowing they had almost had their throats cut.

"Next morning, it was Christmas morning, they started out and Jarvis was pulling rear security. The ARVN was back there with him. They were following a trail through the elephant grass, and waitaminute bushes …"

"I hate those waitaminute bushes," Mundy said. "They do nothing but slow you down."

"They were making their way down the trail, when they heard voices coming up from behind again," Shaner continued. "Jarvis lets the others know, and they pulled off the trail, and set up an ambush. Jarvis and the ARVN were the first ones to encounter the people coming up on them. They were about 5 or 6 feet off the trail, but there was no cover because of the dryness of the bushes. Jarvis had a CAR-15, and an M-79 with a buckshot round in the chamber …"

"Those buckshot rounds are about as useless as it gets," I said. "I once saw a load of buckshot bounce off a C-ration can."

"Hell, I bet they would even bounce off a bag of LRP Rations." Mundy added.

"The ARVN had an M-1 carbine with a 30 round clip." Shaner continues. "They were setting down leaning on their packs waiting, weapons at the ready, and a small boy walked by, and stopped right in front of them. He had a White Phosphorus grenade in his hand. The boy stopped and turned, he looked right at them. He was a Yard in a loincloth, and a GI shirt. Jarvis had his finger on the trigger, but the kid had no gun and he was a little boy …"

"He had that grenade, that was dangerous enough." Mundy said

"The kid turned to the people behind him and said something in Yard, and walked on up the trail," Shaner said. "Then a man walked up to the same spot the boy had stood, and turned just as the boy had, but he had a M-1 carbine slung on his left shoulder he started to unsling his weapon, and so Jarvis opened up on him. The VC started to yell, and managed to get his weapon off his shoulder and to fire back. The other VC were yelling and firing too. Our guys were yelling, asking what was happening. Jarvis managed to change magazine in my CAR-15. He got off one round from the new magazine when the CAR-15 jammed …"

"Oh, shit," Neugard said. "What a time to have a jam."

"He thought he was dead with all that was happening just six feet away," Shaner said. "He figured the only way out was to run away through the wait-a-minute bushes. He started to run and could see the leaves next to him being shot up by this VC. He didn't run very far because the bushes were thick. By that time the guy he shot took off toward the rest of our guys, and they opened up on him as he ran by. He fell down, got up again, and ran in to the bushes. They never found his body. The other VC got away.

"The Team Leader, and ATL lost it. They were white as sheets, and couldn't do a thing but shake. Jarvis actually took over running the team, he told the RTO to call, and get them out of there …"

"At least someone kept their cool," Mundy said.

"He told the Team Leader to pull security but it was no use, the guy was too afraid. Jarvis' weapon was still jammed. He told the Team Leader to give him his weapon but he wouldn't let go of it. So, Jarvis ended up guarding the extraction with a jammed weapon."

"How did a guy like that ever get to be a Team Leader?" I asked.

"This was his first mission," Shaner said. "He got to be Team Leader because he was an E-6. That mission may have taught us that when it comes to leading a Lerp Team, experience is more important than rank."

"Two Bravo, this is Bikini Four Two, do you read me? Over." The radio brought us back to the reality that there was another Christmas contact going on.

"Roger, Bikini Four Two, you're coming in lima charley but we don't hear your rotor blades yet. Over."

"We're still about four klicks from your AO. Have you returned to the same position where you were at zero, one hundred hours? Over."

"Negative, we're about two hundred yards south of that location. We're on a large rock about a third of the way across the blue line, over."

"Any sign of the bad guys? Over."

"Roger, about ten minutes ago we saw some flashlights, and heard voices about a hundred meters south of us. We hear your rotors now, it sounds like you're coming in from the northeast. Over."

I looked around the bar. No one was seated at the tables. Everyone was at the bar crowded around the PRC-25, hanging on every word.

"I'm now on the blue line turning south. If you can give me a strobe light I've got a couple of guys escorting me that can keep the bad guys busy, over."

"Roger, Bikini Four Two, it's going on now."

"I have your location, and we're coming in, over." As he spoke the words the distinct whirring of rapid firing mini guns could be heard over the flip, flip of the rotor blades. Then the radio again went silent. The pilot had released his radio key.

"Those guys are good," Shaner said. "I wish they had been around when I was running missions."

Tension gripped the Bunker Bar. No one spoke. Drinks went unattended. All ears were cocked toward the silent radio. Time drug on. How long did it take for a helicopter to come in, and for four men to climb to safety? A nervous cough from someone within the bar did nothing to relieve the tension. Three, four, five minutes passed. What was happening?

Then the radio came alive again as the pilot broke squelch. "Seven Niner Charley, this is Bikini Four Two. We have your Lima Romeo Papa Team safe and sound. We're bringing them home. Over."

The cheers from everyone in the bar drowned out Seven Niner Charlie's reply. Mundy reached over and shut off the radio.

A week later, New Years Eve found me in the field. As midnight approached we received a radio message that the Fourth Division was cannonballing. In other words, every radio frequency in the entire Division was being changed on the stroke of midnight. They sent our new frequency in code. There is no worse time for LRPs to have to decode a new radio frequency than at midnight, it is pitch black and you dare not light a flashlight, or even a match, for fear that it will be seen. So it was that I brought in the New Year of 1969 huddled under a doubled over poncho liner decoding our new frequency by the light of a cigarette.

13

The New Year

Thursday January 2, 1969

Dear Diary,

Just back from a mission. Guess I should make a New Years resolution. I'll resolve to be a better LRP. I wonder what the New Year will bring …

The first thing that the year 1969 brought in was a new Platoon Sergeant. He came from the 1st of the 12th Infantry to finish his tour of duty with the LRPs. Even now, more than thirty years after that January day, when I picture the ideal Platoon Sergeant the image of Clyde Hinkle comes to mind. He was a big man, probably, at that time, in his early forties. He had a gruff voice laced with sarcasm, and a mastery of army life gained by trial and error. Many men are called leaders, few deserve the title; Sergeant Hinkle was one that did.

I don't remember when I first met him, but I got to know him over a poker table in the Bunker Bar. He played poker in the same manner that he ran the platoon, no nonsense, by the book. But, by a book that he knew so well, the one where he understood which rules could be bent, and how far he could bend them. All Platoon Sergeants know that their job is to take orders from officers and make them happen. Sergeant Hinkle knew that the job also entailed figuring out what was best for the men—and making that happen too.

The antithesis of Sergeant Hinkle, the man who would be a thorn in his side, arrived two weeks later in the form of our new Executive Officer. My disdain for officers, gained by association with incompetent training officers in my ten weeks at OCS, had somewhat abated through my friendlier association with two of them over the bridge table. Lieutenant Railwood would eventually undo all that Lieutenant Miller and his friend had done to ameliorate my attitude toward officers.

In a way you've already met Lt. Railwood. He was the one that wouldn't extract me when I had been stung by centipedes. Rumors soon spread that he had been with a line company, but had been kicked out after an incident where he had sent out a squad to serve as a listening post, then, hearing noises in the night, had fired on the very men he had sent out. But, it was all rumors. The truth was he was new in country, fresh from the replacement depot, filled with attitude, bereft of brains.

A clash between the two was inevitable. The fact was that it was only one clash, but it lasted from the time Railwood walked onto Firebase Mary Lou until Sergeant Hinkle's date of rotation nearly five months later. It didn't divide the platoon, the men didn't let it, but in Railwood's mind it was divided between those that were there before he arrived, and those that came later. To him, those that were already there were Hinkle's friends, and those that came later, most of whom he had recruited, were beholding to him. The fact was, I knew no one that disliked Hinkle, no matter when they came, and no one who felt beholding to Railwood, whether or not he had recruited them.

Except for his haughty demeanor you could almost feel sorry for Railwood. His tussle with Hinkle was an uneven match. Though he was an officer, and Hinkle a NCO, he found little support from his fellow officers, and none from the enlisted ranks. He was out thought, out maneuvered, and rebuffed every time he tried to exert authority beyond his assigned duties. But, any pity I felt for him in those early days died away when, in later months, the true level of his incompetence and vindictiveness became apparent.

Hinkle's primary weapon was his incredible knowledge of Army Regulations. I witnessed this tactic in use the night when a fire broke out on Mary Lou. Hinkle was organizing the LRPs that were in camp to do our part in fighting the fire, when Railwood burst upon the scene, and began ordering soldiers to do this and that in a helter-skelter fashion. In an instant Hinkle was in his face.

"Back up young Lieutenant, Sir," he said poking his index finger into Railwood's chest for emphasis.

"You don't have the authority to give such orders. Army Regulations six, one, one, dash three, Chapter seven, dash one, Section A, two, prohibits an officer from usurping the duties of a Sergeant in authority, when such a Sergeant is on the scene. You can tell me to fight this fire, you can tell me how you want this fire fought, but you can't tell me how to organize these men. Look it up!"

Railwood was humiliated. He saw that I was only five feet away, and had heard every word. I must have had some sort of a grin on my face, because from that day forward I seemed to be second only to Hinkle on Railwood's list of enemies.

14

A Jug of Wine and a Cow

Sunday January 5, 1969

Dear Diary,

Our next mission is supposed to be a stay behind mission. We will go in with another outfit and stay behind when they leave to see if anybody is following them.

Some times men and their means of transportation just naturally seemed to go together. Where would Gene Autry be without Champion? Roy Rogers without Trigger? Batman without the Batmobile? Or for that matter, LRPs without helicopters? Just once in my time in Vietnam I ran a mission that didn't involve helicopters. It was called a stay behind mission. We would go in with a platoon of Armored Personnel Carriers, and remain behind to see if they were followed by the bad guys

The team leader was Crowder, the other team members were Price and Jackson. We rode with the mechanized infantry men on the top of an Armored Personnel Carrier, or APC, as they were called. It was designed for people to ride inside, but the walls were so thin that a machine gun could penetrate the armor, and rattle around the inside hitting more than one occupant. Most GIs felt safer on top. If you were on top you could jump off and hide in the bush, or get behind the APC where the shot would have to penetrate both armored walls.

The thing that stuck me most was the noise. Sure helicopters made noise, but most of the time they flew high enough to be out of range, and when close to the ground, fast enough to be a hard target. The APC was noisy, slow and stuck to the ground. On top of the noise of the engine and the clanking of the treads was the crashing, and thrashing of small trees, and brush as they were pushed down by the powerful machines. It didn't seem like a very good way to fight a jungle war.

We weren't far from Mary Lou, traveling through a patch of jungle that was near a Montagnard village. Not since leaving Bam Me Thuot had I run a mission in such close proximity to native civilians. I was uncomfortable because of it, believe it or not, there was something secure about being out in the middle of nowhere, with nobody but bad guys about. Some villagers could be Viet Cong, or even if they weren't, if they knew you were there they could let it slip to someone who was.

They dropped us off about halfway through the patch of jungle. We set up on the uphill side about 15 yards from the down-beaten trail left by the APCs. Slowly their noise subsided. After five minutes the clanking and thrashing seemed as loud as when they left, after ten minutes a distant rumble, finally, after fifteen minutes the noise of the slow moving leviathans disappeared into the distance. Now we waited, watching the trail and listening for the subtler noises of sandal clad feet, and words spoken softly in an alien tongue. One hour, two hours and then three, and no one came. The tracks weren't being followed. So, in that time we had completed our primary mission, it now became just a normal reconnaissance mission.

Crowder determined that our ambush location would also make a good night location. We fixed our rations and settled in for the night. On the next day we would inspect our Area of Operations.

After an uneventful night we set out on our reconnaissance of our AO. Unlike most areas of operation, which were four square kilometers, this AO was one kilometer wide and two long. As we had covered the first of our two kilometers on the back of the APC, we were left with only one to cover. We did that in a day.

The western edge of the AO was open farm and grazing land, and provided a continuous LZ for a helicopter extraction. We followed the western wood line back across the AO, skirting the open fields. By mid afternoon we were confident that no overt enemies were in the area. Covert ones, however, in the form of the native inhabitants were a definite possibility.

Crowder found what appeared to be an excellent night location. It was a thick bush right on the edge of an open field used by Montagnard farmers as a cow pasture. We crawled in, cut out our sleeping area from the inside of the bush, and settled in for a quiet night.

I woke in the morning to the smell of coffee, and rattling of a canteen cup on a tin can stove. Jackson had the last watch, and when daylight settled in he was fixing his breakfast. I rubbed the sleep from my eyes, and lit a cigarette. Crowder was awake and digging a LRP ration out of his pack. Price was just beginning to stir. We each took our turn with the tin can stove boiling enough water to mix with our LRP Rations, and still have enough left to pour in a packed of army coffee, and a packet or two of sugar. Instead of coffee Price chose instead a packet of instant cocoa.

We were still sipping on our hot drinks, and smoking when out of nowhere the entrance of our hiding place was pulled apart. Four hearts nearly stopped. Our heads snapped in panic toward the opening. A grinning Montagnard face appeared between the hands that had spread open the gap. If it had been an enemy we would have been dead, caught totally off guard and shot down before we could grab our weapons. But instead he merely smiled, nodded his head, and spoke some unintelligible words to an unseen companion.

We, who thought ourselves the masters of stealth, had been caught unaware by two peasant farmers. We crawled out from the spot where we felt we had been so well hidden to confront the intruders. In broken pidgin with many a gesture the farmers explained that they were checking on their cattle when they heard noises, and smelled smells coming from the bush. They appeared very friendly and pleasant, and except for walking sticks, were unarmed. We explained that we were there looking for VC and they told us that VC were very bad, but were also long gone from the area.

Thus we parted on friendly terms the farmers going on with their business, and we crawling back into our very compromised hiding place. We told ourselves that we must be more careful, but, unfortunately, soon resumed our careless ways. Crowder made no attempt to move the team. We had checked out the AO, and found no signs of enemy activity. I lit another cigarette, we finished our coffee and continued to talk about things in a hushed whisper.

A couple of hours later history repeated itself. The bushes suddenly parted, and our farmer's friendly face appeared in the opening. This was getting embarrassing. Crowder tried to tell the man that what he was doing was very dangerous. If we heard movement close to us we might start shooting, not realizing it was him. He just smiled nodded, and pushed forward a large earthenware jug. Crowder reached out, and took it. The farmer began to babble, partly in Pidgin English, partly in Vietnamese and partly in French. We could only make out a small portion of what he was saying. He explained that it was a gift, Montagnard rice wine. We were to drink it through the bamboo straw that extended from the jug. If we ran out we were not to worry, all we had to do was to add water and let it sit for a few minutes, and we would have more. We thanked him profusely, and he went on his way.

We set the jug in the middle of our night location. Crowder took a long pull on the bamboo straw. "You know this stuff's pretty good," he said.

He passed the straw and we all joined in. It didn't take long to get down to the fermented rice that covered the bottom of the jug.

"Hey, were out of the stuff," Jackson said.

"What did he say," Crowder said. "All we have to do is to add more water and the rice would make more wine."

"I've got three canteens left," I said. "I'll contribute one to the cause.

"Me too," Price said.

So it was decided that we would each contribute a canteen of water to add to the jug.

We let it sit for no more than five minutes before Crowder took a sip to sample its progress. "That stuff is just like it was before. Adding water really works!"

"You know," I said, "If we could figure out how to do this back in the States our fortune would be made."

"How do you figure?" Crowder said.

"Instant booze, every wino in the country would give their last nickel for it."

"It's not very strong," Jackson said.

"It doesn't have to be if there is enough quantity," I said.

I was beginning to feel a slight buzz from the stuff, and from the look of my companions they were further gone than I was. We crawled out of our bush and stood up. It was a nice little field, marked on the far side by a rail fence. It was late afternoon and eight or ten cows were grazing about twenty yards from us.

"That stuff is sort of like pot," Price said. "I've got the munchies."

"It would be nice to have something other that LRP Rations," Crowder said.

"Well there's steak on the hoof over there," I said pointing to the cattle.

"Yeah, but who knows how to butcher them?" Price said.

"I've seen it done, but I've never done it," I said. "My brother used to work as a butcher, in a processing plant back home. After you shoot them you've got to take a sharp knife and cut their juggler to bleed them. Then you cut them open and remove the guts."

"Like that knife of yours," Price said.

"It's not what they would use in the States, but it would do in a pinch."

"I'm a city boy," Price said, "I wouldn't even know a good one to shoot. Is that one any good?" He pointed to an older cow. He was definitely a city boy. He was pointing at a full grown cow.

"City guys used to come out to country to go deer hunting. There wasn't a goat or mule in the country that was safe from a city guy with a gun." I said. "No, that wouldn't be any good, it's old enough to be tough." I pointed to a yearling, "That heifer there, would be the best one in the batch."

I had barely finished the sentence, and had not yet lowered my arm when I heard the crack of a rifle. I turned to see Price with the butt of his M-16 still to his shoulder.

"Got it," he said.

The cow fell on its haunches, its front legs still trying to pull itself forward.

"You shot it in the ass!" I said.

"You didn't tell me you had to shoot it someplace special."

The cow finally lost its footing, and fell on its side. I ran to it and put it out of its misery with a bullet through its brain. I pulled out my knife and tried to slice its throat to cut the juggler vein. The knife really was sharp, it could cut most anything I could imagine, but it couldn't cut through that beasts hide.

"Damn," I said. "I can't cut through this thing. We've got to get rid of it before the farmer finds out we shot his cow."

The others grabbed the hind legs, and I grabbed the front legs, we dragged it over to the edge of the field, and deposited it behind the rail fence. It wasn't very well disguised, but maybe we would be gone before he found it.

We never saw the farmer again. We spent that night in the same compromised location. It didn't seem to bother my compadres, but I didn't sleep well. I don't know how long it took the farmer to locate his missing cow, in the heat of Vietnam probably not long. But he didn't come, and he didn't send the Vietcong.

The next morning we learned that no helicopters were available to extract us and if we wanted to go home we would have to walk. We packed up our gear and began to walk. The jug of rice wine fit comfortably into Jackson's pack, with the bamboo straw sticking conspicuously out from beneath the flap. We humped to the main road and, maybe a mile further when Cueball, the platoon driver, came along in the Jeep, and drove us the rest of the way home.

The jug of rice wine made Jackson quite a hit for two or three days. After that the fermented rice lost its potency and had to be thrown out. I never did learn how it was made, though I remain convinced that there would be a commercial future for instant booze.

At the end of January all LRP units in Vietnam were incorporated into the 75th Infantry Rangers. Our new address was 2nd Brigade, Ranger Platoon. At the Division level, E Company 58th Infantry LRPs became K Company 75th Infantry Rangers. Being a Ranger didn't change a thing. Most of us still thought of ourselves as LRPs. We figured that the Rangers just wanted a record in the Vietnam War, and that they couldn't do any better than to take ours.

It was also at the end of January that I took my out of country R and R. I spent a week wallowing in drunken debauchery in Yokohama, Japan. After finding a cheap hotel three other guys and I hailed a taxi and told him to take us to where there were women. He took us to a bar that catered to GIs on R and R. We paid Mamasan, who owned the bar, and the girls came back to the hotel with us. My girl was named Connie. Her hair was dyed blond, and she applied her makeup in such a way as to look as American as possible. I would have preferred her natural Asian look, but among GIs I was in the minority in that regard. She was pretty, though, and definitely willing. I brought a thousand dollars with me. Connie got most of it. I spent another one or two hundred on food and booze. The rest I wasted.

I've never felt guilty about my drunkenness and whoring. But, even now, after all these years I still have some feelings of guilt. I truly believe that when my time comes to stand before the seat of judgement, I will have to answer for my part in senseless murder of some poor farmer's cow, in Kontum Province, in Vietnam, in January 1969.

15

Festus Runs into Trouble

Wednesday January 23, 1969

Dear Diary,

Just back from R&R and am suffering the consequences of my profligate life. I've got to go to the infirmary just as soon as it opens …

The Bible says that the wages of sin are death, but, evidently, the sins I committed during R and R weren't so great that they couldn't be cured by three massive doses of Penicillin, shot into my ass, on three successive days. It was on my third visit to the infirmary that I ran into Quintero. Quintero was Puerto Rican, and one of the best LRPs in the platoon. He was lean, with a dark complexion, and a pencil thin moustache.

"What's up?" he asked.

"Not much," I said. "I'm just here to get a shot of Penicillin."

"I got to get some stuff for athletes foot," he said.

"Lucky you," I said.

"You had more fun getting what you got. You know," he said changing the subject, "a strange thing, I come in here the other day, and in the outer room they are interrogating a captured North Vietnamese. After I walk through, I come in here to wait to see the Doctor. Ten minutes later this Captain comes in and thanks me.

"'Why do you thank me,' I say to him.

"He says, 'Before you come through that NVA soldier is shut up like a clam. You come through in your Tiger fatigues and Lerp hat, and he starts talking and he hasn't shut up since. He's afraid that we will give him to you.'"

"It sounds like they have heard of us," I said.

"Sure they have," Quintero said. "That's why they have a $1,500 price on our head, we are tough guys."

"Speaking of tough guys," I said, "I saw our buddy Festus when I was in Pleiku getting ready to go on R and R."

"How's he doing?"

"He's doing fine, he's with the First Brigade Lerps now."

"Does he like it there?"

"It's hard to say. He thinks they're too soft." I said. "He thinks we've gone soft too. Hell, he even thinks the Green Beret's have gone soft. He says next time around he might join the Navy SEALS."

"He just needs a good contact to stir up his blood," Quintero said.

"Evidently he's had at least one," I said. "He told me that his team ran into a company of NVA, and they started after him. He called in artillery on his own position then ran for it. Then he dropped tear gas on his trail, but they kept on coming. Finally they spread out, and started to surround them. Luckily gun ships arrived, and kept the bad guys at bay.

"But, before long the gun ships began to use up their munitions, and to peel off to return to their base to reload. Finally there was only one chopper left. The pilot called down to Festus, 'more birds are on their way, but I've only got enough ammunition for one more pass,' he said. 'What do you want, point three-eights or point four-fives?'

"Now, Festus had never heard of either rockets, or mini-gun ammo designated in that way, but point four-five sounded bigger. 'Give me the point four-five!' Festus told him.

"The chopper swings down low over the enemy, and both the pilot and co-pilot have their arms out the window, and they're shooting forty-five automatic pistols at the bad guys. Festus didn't think that those guys hadn't gotten too soft."

The Doctor called me next, ending the conversation. I got my shot, and clearance to begin running missions again. Two days later I had a new team, and was headed out for a new adventure.

16

Neugard Gets his Nose Pierced

Saturday January 25, 1969

Dear Diary,

Got a new team. Neugard is on it. I haven't been on a mission with any of the guys I came here with since the missions with Murphy and Torres.

In these times it's not unusual to see a guy with his ears, nose, tongue, eyebrows, or most any other part of his body, pierced. Even back in the sixties, with the hippies and all, piercing wasn't unheard of. But a guy with a pierced nose who has a GI haircut, and is wearing camouflaged fatigues, and when that guy is Neugard, the consummate straight arrow, now that's a different story. Here's what happened.

We were looking for bad guys in the Plei Trap Valley. Massoletti was the Team Leader. This was my first mission with him. Though I didn't know it then, there would be several more. On my list of the giants from whom I learned, none ranks higher than Massoletti. In truth, I had more missions than he had, but he had more time in country. He was a Sergeant that had come from a line outfit, and had moved quickly into a Team Leader slot. He was the epitome of the all American boy, blond curly hair, and blue eyes. He looked like a hero, and, like Roy Rogers or Gene Autry, seemed to come through the toughest fight without a hair out of place, or a speck of dirt on his tiger fatigues.

Renn walked point for Massoletti. He was a lean, red headed country boy, rather quiet, but a good soldier who could be depended on to do his job. Neugard was Assistant Team Leader. By this time he had his own team but, like me, he was just back off R & R. His team had been reassigned in his absence. Neugard had developed into a very good LRP, but did have one slight bad habit. He was just a little bit accident prone—or, maybe—just a little unlucky. He wasn't a danger to be around; he was more of a danger to himself. For example he was once leading his team when he spotted some pungy stakes along the trail. Pungy stakes were sharpened bamboo spikes, often urinated on so that they would cause infection. The VC and NVA would dig pits and fill them with pungy stakes and cover them with twigs and grass as a booby trap, or would set them in the ground along a trail. Neugard turned to warn his team to be careful, and promptly drove one of the stakes through his boot, and into his foot.

As usual I walked rear security. It was on our second day out, if I remember correctly, that we began to descend the hill into the heavily jungled valley below. I liked hills, I liked being on hills. Hills gave you the high ground, and were usually close to landing zones. Valleys were a different story; bad things happened in valleys. The V.C. and N.V.A. liked to hang out in valleys, and when you went into a valley you almost always lost radio communications with your base camp. We hadn't gone far when Massoletti turned, and whispered that we had lost radio commo. I wondered what else would go wrong.

When we reached the floor of the valley we found a broad well used trail. Massoletti decided to follow the trail. Have I mentioned that I don't like trails? The bad guys who hang out in valleys, tend to walk on trails in those valleys. We hadn't gone more than twenty yards down the trail when Renn stopped, and signaled Massoletti forward. Then Massoletti signaled Neugard and me, and we all gathered around looking down at the foot print made by a Ho Chi Min sandal, the distinct footwear of the Vietcong.

Massoletti pointed to a small piece of white cloth a few feet on the other side of the footprint. There were four or five spots of blood on it.

"Do you think he's wounded?" Neugard whispered.

"If so it's not much of a wound," I said. "It looks more like a scratch or a nose bleed."

"I'd prefer it to be something more serious," Massoletti said.

A Team Leader is called on to make a lot of decisions, team members do not always agree with those decisions, but we followed along, because he was the leader. This time Massoletti made a decision that I totally agreed with. He decided to find out where the wearer of that sandal had come from, rather than where he was going.

"There's got to be one less bad guy that way than there is where ever he went to," I whispered to Renn.

Before long we came to a broad shallow stream, maybe fifteen yards across, and, at its deepest spot, no more than two feet in depth. We slogged across the stream, soaking our pants legs up to the knees, and set up on the other side in a small cluster of trees a few yards off the trail. Massoletti got out the long antenna for the PRC-25, and tried again to establish commo. He still couldn't get hold of base camp, but he did reach an airforce FAC that was roaming the area. A few seconds later we heard the drone of the engines, and saw the plane approaching.

"The pilot wants to know our location," Massoletti whispered. "Neugard, go down to the creek and flash him a mirror."

Neugard grabbed his CAR-15, and headed for the bank of the creek. He took his signal mirror from his breast pocket, caught the sun, and flashed it against the side of the plane.

Now, in this world there are many bad shots, but I have to hold that in any ranking of bad shots the Vietcong come in second worst. They are slightly worse than the North Vietnamese, both having shot at me and missed, and though I pride myself in being a good shot I have to admit I am a better target, and, as proven by the eventual outcome of the war, slightly better than the South Vietnamese. The Vietcong that stepped out onto the riverbank across from Neugard must have been a contender for worst shot among the Vietcong. Neugard on his side of the bank saw the black pajama clad figure out of the corner of his eye, and, while still trying to steady the mirror on the FAC, was reaching behind himself trying to find where he had laid his CAR-15. The V.C. raised the SKS rifle he was carrying, and fired all five rounds from the magazine. He didn't come close to hitting Neugard, but one of the bullets, one solitary bullet, hit a rock that was jutting out of the river, and a piece of that rock, a shard no larger than a grain of sand, broke away from the rock and became a piece of shrapnel. It shot toward Neugard, up his left nostril and out the side of his nose.

Now, I have already told you that the water in that river was two feet deep, that it wet our pants legs up to the knee, but I am here to swear that I saw Neugard re-cross that river, CAR-15 in hand, at a dead run, going after the Vietcong that had shot him, and I never saw his feet break the surface of the water. Neugard was ticked!

He crouched down on the other bank and waited for that V.C. to stick his head up. Meanwhile, Massoletti reported the contact to the Forward Air Controller, and slipped part way down the bank to assume a better defensive position. I picked up the horn and, because I was the only one who could actually see Neugard, reported his condition, and requested a Dustoff. Renn had taken up a position watching the rear, and guarding against anyone coming down the trail from the other direction.

Every once in a while Neugard would take a handful of river water to wash away the copious amounts of blood that poured from that little hole in his nose, or he would wipe the blood away with his sleeve, but mostly he stared steadily at the brush looking for his adversary.

"He doesn't appear to be badly injured," I reported to the FAC, "but he's bleeding profusely."

Massoletti had a good position behind a tree that was growing close to the water's edge, but he couldn't see Neugard.

"Neugard are you all right!" he shouted across the water. Neugard raised his finger to his lips, and then flattened out his palm and pushed downward on the air to emphasize that we should keep quiet.

"He says he's all right, but that we should keep quiet," I whispered across to Massoletti. But, Massoletti was to excited to hear LRP whispers, his ears were attuned to noises from across the river.

"Neugard, are you all right!" he shouted again.

Again the gestures from Neugard, and again my whisper, this time somewhat louder than before.

"He says he's all right. He's trying to get the guy that shot him—keep it down."

Massoletti wasn't listening. "Neugard are you all right!" he shouted a third time.

"SHUT UP, BITCH!" came Neugard's reply at the top of his lungs.

"I told you he was okay," I said. This time, seeing no further need to whisper, in a normal tone of voice.

When, in a few more minutes the V.C. had not reappeared, Massoletti gave orders for us to provide cover fire for Neugard's return to our side of the river. He peppered the opposite bank up stream with fire from his CAR—15, and I popped M-79 rounds on the down stream side. Neugard's return passage was not nearly so swift, and his feet sank once more to a normal depth.

The FAC pilot directed us to the nearest LZ. Neugard trotted along between Massoletti, and me holding a bandage against his nose. Massoletti kept the radio handset to his ear as we moved.

"The pilot said that he's getting heavy machine gun fire from that hill over there." He pointed with his handset to the hill we had not long before descended. Maybe hills weren't such safe places after all.

Neugard was evacuated by Dustoff, the Army's medical evacuation helicopter corps, the other three of us had to wait an extra twenty minutes for the regular extraction slicks.

Cueball, was waiting at the landing pad with a jeep. He took us up the hill to the platoon area. Sergeant Hinkle greeted us when we got to the HQ tent to return our gear.

"That was you on the radio that reported Neugard's condition, wasn't it?" he said to me as we entered.

"Yeah, I guess so," I said. "Why?"

"Well, you're the only one I know that would tell the FAC pilot that Neugard was 'bleeding profusely.'"

17

What a Deal!

Lt. Railwood found himself a deal. He could get a minigun for a case of booze. He knew we didn't need a minigun. Where would we put it? I guess we could have put it on the back of Cueball's Jeep, but then where would we ride, and where would you carry enough ammunition. At slow fire a six barreled minigun fired at 1500 rounds a minute, if you cranked it up all the way, like they did on the C-47 airplanes they called Spookies (or in some areas Jolly Green Giants) they fired at 3000 rounds a minute. Even if it wasn't full of LRPs, the back of Cueball's Jeep wasn't big enough to carry enough ammunition for more than a minutes shooting. No, a minigun was not practical for a LRP Platoon, but what a deal, a minigun for a case of booze.

The case of booze was, of course, requisitioned from the Bunker Bar. As most of the guys drank beer, that case of booze would have lasted a couple of months for those of us that liked the hard stuff. We had paid for it too; we had all chipped in to buy the first batch from the Green Beret's. But Lt. Railwood was not to be dissuaded. He got his case of booze and he got his minigun.

"A fine weapon, in excellent condition," Sgt. Hinkle told him when he showed it off in the Headquarters tent. Railwood's chest started to swell with pride in expectation of praise from his arch enemy. Then Hinkle released his acid tongue.

"What are you going to do with it?" He said "We're not on the perimeter, so we can't put it on a tower. We've got one Jeep, to haul teams back and forth to the helipad. We can't mount a mini-gun on the Jeep. And what if there's an I.G. Inspection? We're not authorized a minigun. What are we going to do when the next I. G. Inspection happens? Are we going to dig a hole and bury it? It takes a pretty big hole to bury a minigun, and that kind of hole would be a lot harder to camouflage."

Railwood was not about to let Hinkle top him in his moment of glory. "That's the beauty of it," he said. "We don't need to keep it. I can trade it to the Special Forces. The Green Beret will probably give us a lot of stuff in trade."

That's how Lt. Railwood started his trading expedition to the local Special Forces camp. He loaded the minigun into the back of a duce and a half, and headed for the Special Forces, C and C Camp that was a couple of miles from Mary Lou. He took a half dozen of us enlisted men to help him haul back his booty.

Most of the guys would jump at the chance whenever they needed volunteers to go to the C and C Camp. The Green Beret knew how to live when they were in Base Camp. They had a real NCO club, made of brick, not sandbags, and equipped with a real bar, complete with brass rail. Their mess hall always served steak, and was open any time of day. It was a grunt's dream of paradise, and even a LRP appreciated the additional creature comforts. But, this trip was with Lt. Railwood. We were ordered to stay with the duce and a half while he went off to find someone with whom to bargain.

We waited in the back of the open duce and a half. It was hot. Our LRP hats were the only protection from the tropical sun. It was an hour maybe more before Railwood reappeared and climbed in next to the driver. He directed us around to the back of the building where he gave up the minigun, and received in return three Swedish K submachine guns, and ten pillows. They didn't make a very big pile in the bed of the duce and a half.

As I already had a pillow, I grabbed one of the Swedish Ks. After all I had a stake in this deal; some of the money that had bought that case of booze came from my pocket. The submachine gun was brand new, still wrapped for shipping. On the way back to Mary Lou I opened the package. Inside was a twenty-two inch long gray weapon, with a folding stock attached to a wooden pistol grip. When unfolded it lengthened the weapon by another ten inches. A magazine that would hold thirty-six, 9 mm rounds was lying next to the receiver. The package also contained a leather magazine case with ten more magazines.

I now had all the weaponry I needed. From now on when I went to the field I would have a 38 derringer in a shoulder holster under my shirt; a British Commando Knife would be taped horizontally to the back of my web belt; Canteen pouches hung onto the belt would contain fragmentation, white phosphorus and M-79 grenades; My M-79 would be tied to my back pack, the leather magazine case would be hung around my neck and left arm so that it covered the left side of my chest; the Swedish K, its' stock folded would be hung from it's long, leather strap around my neck so that I could hold it by the pistol grip and magazine and sweep it in a wide arc. So armed and equipped I felt like, and looked like, one mean dude.

As our previous mission had been cut short, we were at Mary Lou for longer than normal, and I had a chance to try out my new weapon. Though other LRPs might disagree, and maintain their advocacy of the CAR-15, to my mind the Swedish K was the perfect weapon for jungle fighting. The magazine was large enough to lay down a sustained blanket of fire. It weighed nearly ten pounds, three pounds of which was the bolt. This meant that you could fire it fully automatic, which was in fact the only way you could fire it, without the muzzle rise experienced with the M-16 and CAR-15. The 9 mm pistol ammunition it used made a lot bigger hole than the 5.56 mm rounds for the M-16. It didn't have long range accuracy, but in the jungle you would seldom make contact with the enemy beyond 50 yards, and at 50 yards I could put all 36 rounds into a sixty gallon drum.

18

The Giants Are All Gone

Sunday February 16, 1969

Dear Diary,

This may be one of the worst days yet. So much has been lost. I thought I'd built up a wall against this sort of thing, but I guess it didn't work …

After my target practice I disassembled my new weapon and gave it a thorough cleaning. When I was satisfied that it was ready to take on the NVA, I reassembled it, and was taking it back to the armory. I had to go to the headquarters tent to get the key to the padlock on the steel door. Sgt. Hinkle was on the phone talking to BTOC. He looked troubled.

"I'm on my way to the helipad now," he said and hung up the phone. Cueball and I were the only ones with him in the tent. "Cueball get the Jeep, Reed spread the word, we've got a team in trouble we may need to go in after them. Send everybody you can down to the helipad."

"Which team?" Cueball and I said nearly in unison.

"Two Delta, Hancock's team."

These were the words we both feared.

"The helicopter reported being shot at on insertion. We've had no word since then." As he talked he put on his web gear and grabbed his M-16. "Get moving." He said.

We rushed to our assignments. There weren't many guys in camp. Half the platoon was in the field, others were on over flights and some had gone into town. I went first to the Bunker Bar, most of the guys would be there. I ran down the stairs and pushed open the door. It took my eyes a minute to adjust to the dimly lit room. When I could see, I noticed about a dozen guys in the room.

They were, for the most part, the latest batch of FNGs. I'd seen them around but didn't really know them.

"We've got a team down, and in trouble," I said. "They need us to go in after them. We're meeting at the helipad."

My words were met with blank stares. Nobody moved. Nobody said a word. I backed out into the daylight and headed for the tents. I got the same reaction as I went from tent to tent. A few, mostly guys that had been around for a while, nodded and started to get their gear together, but most just stared at me, and said, and did nothing. Didn't they understand? LRPs were in trouble, it was our duty to go in after them. They would do it for us.

I thought back to Shaner's words about the loss of Finley and Ghahate. "Every Lerp that was here volunteered to help," he had said. "I was real proud of them. All they needed to know was that brother Lerps were in trouble, and they were ready to go." Perhaps Festus was right, we had gotten soft, or maybe it was just that the giants were all gone. We had lost them in the short four months since Finley and Ghahate.

When I got to the helipad only five or six others were there. Sgt. Hinkle and Cueball were sitting in the Jeep. Hinkle had the handset of the Jeeps radio to his ear. Cueball was hunched forward with his forehead against the steering wheel. If there was one person in the platoon closer to Hancock than I, it was Cueball. At the time I didn't know what it was that bonded them together, years later I learned that they were two of the three that had gotten aboard the helicopter on the night when Finley and Ghahate had not.

Hinkle patted Cueball on the back then got out of the Jeep and came over to where the rest of us waited. "It's not a rescue mission anymore," he said. "It's a recovery mission. The back up helicopter landed, and couldn't find anyone alive."

We stood there in stunned silence. I felt all empty inside. My fears were realized. After a minute someone in the group asked, "Who was on the team?"

"Hancock, Dunn, McKinney and Rightmyer," Hinkle said. "There were four helicopter crewmen killed too."

"Were they shot down?" Someone asked.

"The last message from the pilot was that they had been hit by ground fire, and the helicopter was hard to control."

"Sergeant Hinkle, the Major want's to talk to you." Cueball's cracked voice said from the Jeep. He was holding the handset in his hand. Hinkle went to the Jeep and took the horn. He talked little, and listened much. When he was through he came back to where we waited.

"We won't need you after all," he said. "They're sending in an Air Rifle Platoon to secure the area. I've got to go in and identify our guys."

The other LRPs left. Cueball and I waited until a Light Observation Helicopter, called a LOH, flew in and landed on the pad. Hinkle got in and the helicopter took off.

When Hinkle returned I rushed to the HQ tent to find out more. Massoletti was there too. "They didn't have a chance," he told us. "The insertion LZ was the only one in the AO. I don't know if they spent too much time over the AO during the visual reconnaissance, or if the North Vietnamese just guessed that a team was coming in. Not only were they firing at the helicopter, but they had the LZ booby trapped as well. They had cables strung from tree to tree across both ends of the LZ. It would have been almost impossible for the tail rotor not to hit one of them. The second helicopter would have caught it too, except that the helicopter that crashed broke the cable.

"It was a horrible scene," he said. "When the helicopter caught the cable it flipped it over. One of the door gunners fell out, and through the rotor blades. I found his helmet—with his head still in it. Our guys, and the pilot and co-pilot burned in the crash." He choked on the last words, he couldn't talk any more, he just waived his hand for us to go.

Two days after it happened they would hold a ceremony to honor those that had died. On the day before the ceremony I was passing by Hancock's tent when I heard quiet weeping. I looked in, and saw Cueball sitting on Hancock's bunk. He had been packing Hancock's things to send them to his wife, but now he was just sitting there holding a piece of paper in his hand, and crying.

"What's wrong?" I asked.

"Look," he said, handing me the paper. "I found this among Jerry's poems."

I read it, and had to stifle back my own tears. "We've got to get this to Lieutenant Miller," I said. "This has to be part of the ceremony tomorrow."

"But I need to pack it to send to his wife."

"Whether it is in his hand, or not doesn't matter. We'll make copies, and you can pack up the original."

We wrote out three copies of the poem, one for Cueball, one for me, and one to give to the Lieutenant.

"We found this among Hancock's things," I said when we handed the copy to Lt. Miller. "I've done some poetry reading, and would be happy to read it at tomorrow's ceremony."

The Lieutenant read the paper, and thought a minute. "No," he said, "Thank you for your offer, but it would be best coming from me. No, I want to read it myself."

The next day they set up a table on the parade ground. On top of the table were the four best LRP hats in the Platoon, each hat representing one of the four dead LRPs. As I had recently gotten a new hat, mine was one. All the LRPs that were in camp gathered to honor their fallen comrades. There may have been other brass there, I really don't remember. It was more important, to me at least, that we honored our own. The Lieutenant pinned a Purple Heart and a Bronze Star on each hat. He saluted, then took the folded paper from his pocket and read the poem.

I listened as he read the words "… I am the diamond glint on snow … I am the soft star shine at night …" I guess it was a fitting tribute, but it didn't do much to fill the emptiness you feel from the loss of a friend. In the years since, I have seen and heard the poem several times. It is attributed to an anonymous source. I realize that Jerry may not have written it himself, but he loved it enough to put it with his own. I will always associate it with him.

19

Tac-E

Wednesday February 25, 1969

Dear Diary,

Just back from two back to back missions. Like the night I listened in on Finley and Ghahate's contact, I used the radio to follow another team in contact ...

We were on one of those forgettable missions. The only thing memorable about it appeared to be that it was the first mission Massoletti, and I ran with Cookie Plaskett. Over the next six weeks Massoletti, Plaskett and I would form the core of team Two Echo. The fourth member of the team would vary from mission to mission, but the three of us would always be there. On this mission the fourth member of the team was Gamble.

We had wandered around a dead AO for three days. There was no sign of enemy activity, there weren't even any trails. But in this war when your AO was cold, it didn't mean that somewhere else there wasn't another AO that was burning up. In the case at hand some ten or fifteen kilometers away Team Two Charlie was fighting for its life. Ironically, Two Charlie wasn't even looking for bad guys, they had been put on top of a mountain to serve as a radio relay, but the NVA had found them and were making it hot.

"Two Charlie, isn't that Matty's team?" I asked, when Massoletti told us what was going on.

"Yeah, it is," Massoletti said. "My first mission as a LRP was with Matty and Barrio.

Matty was a tall blond surfer type from California whose real name was Mateer. He was one of the regulars in the Bunker Bar, and was best friends with Barrio, a short, Italian, New Yorker. Matty was one of those guys that you felt could handle himself in contact, but you still worried about him. It was too soon after we had buried Hancock and his team. The loss of another team would have been devastating.

Late in the morning or our third day Massoletti got a call from Seven Niner Charlie. Matty and his team had been safely extracted, but it had left a communications gap with teams further out. We were to be extracted from the AO we were in and inserted on top of another mountain to take Two Charlie's place. It was only to be for a few days, until a more permanent solution could be worked out. As the birds were already on their way, we had to hump hard to get to the LZ before our transportation.

We made it with just a few minutes to spare. There was a subtle choreography involved in LRP insertions and extractions. There were always four helicopters involved, two Huey transport ships, sometimes called "slicks," and two gunships. The chopper that was to pick you up, or drop you off was always in the lead. It would be followed by a chase ship and flanked by the two gunships. The lead chopper would fly in low over the LZ, then suddenly drop to the ground to pick you up. The chase ship would fly over the ship on the ground, and assume the lead position. Then your bird would take off and assume the chase position. In this way no helicopter would be out of sight for more that a few seconds. Any eyes that were watching for nefarious reasons would, it was hoped, miss the transfer entirely.

They flew us to a mountain a reasonable distance from the one that had been under attack. They landed us on a ridge a couple of hundred yards from the peak. We could tell that the peak had been occupied by GIs in the past. Scattered around the bald knob of the hill were the remnants of bunkers that, due to the erosion of the upper layer of sand bags, were now open to the sky. It wasn't a natural bald knob, the trees and brush had been cut back to give the former occupiers a field of fire.

As we humped the 200 yards to our final destination Plaskett and I began discussing whether this was one or two missions.

"It has to be two separate missions," Plaskett said. "There were two separate insertions and there will have to be two separate extractions."

"I hope so," I said. "I'd hate to spend the rest of the war here."

"You know what I mean."

"Yeah, I know, and I agree it should count for two missions. But what we think doesn't matter much, the brass back at Mary Lou will count it however they choose."

"But, it will make a difference in when we get to our twenty-five missions, and are given easy duty."

"I'll believe that when I see it," I said. "I think easy duty is a myth, like the two out-of-country R and Rs I was promised when I joined. That's already been pared back to one out-of-country and one in-country, just like every other GI."

"I still think this is two missions," Plaskett said.

"So do I, for whatever good that will do us."

When we reached the peak of the mountain we set up our radio near one of the sandbag walls. We raised the long antenna and made contact with Mary Lou. They gave us the locations and radio frequencies of the various artillery units in support of the teams in the field, so that we could contact them if a team was in trouble. We decoded the information, and Massoletti assigned us shifts to monitor the radio.

Late that afternoon Massoletti was monitoring the radio. "Roger, we'll expect you." I heard him say.

"Keep your eyes open," he said to the team. "That was a Special Forces C and C team. They've chosen this hill to spend the night. They'll be coming up pretty quick with a platoon of Montagnards, and a platoon of South Vietnamese ARVNs."

Before long they came marching in. The Green Beret's nodded recognition, but didn't stop to talk. They made camp above us, on the very crest of the hill. When we weren't monitoring the radio the LRPs went over and visited with the Montagnard troops. For a change of pace we traded some of our LRP rations for some of their rations. It was a mistake. I ended up with some rice, fish heads, and a horrible smelling sausage. Only the rice had the slightest appeal to an American palate. I ate the ration, mainly so that I could say I had, but I didn't even consider going back for seconds.

We killed time until dark playing Casino with a deck of cards Massoletti had brought with him. We turned in feeling a bit more secure than usual, knowing that if any trouble came there would be eighty rifles to respond.

Plaskett woke me at 4 A.M. for my turn on watch. It was a beautiful night. Being on top of a bald hill we were that much closer to the stars, with no jungle foliage masking the view. I sat with my ear to the handset listening for reports from the outlying teams, and watching the glories of the universe. One by one the teams called in their hourly situation reports, in each case all was quiet, and one by one I relayed the information to Seven Niner Charlie. Before too long streaks of gray and then streaks of blue, began to brush away the myriad of stars as dawn invaded the sky. Now the sunshine reports began to come in from the teams and I, dutifully, transmitted them to Mary Lou.

The camp above us was now astir. When I had accounted for all the teams I turned up the volume on the radio, and set it, along with my watch, on a log about five feet from where I sat. I got my canteen cup and some coffee from my pack, and located the tin can stove. My breakfast would be coffee, and a Hershey's jungle chocolate bar.

If the camp above had eaten breakfast it must have been a quick one, because as I was taking my first sips of coffee the Green Berets began to lead their charges back down off the hill. The rest of the LRPs were now beginning to stir too. As I was bidding Plaskett good morning out of the corner of my eye, I saw a Montagnard break rank, and come toward us. He walked up to the log and picked up my watch. Then he walked around the log and came up to me.

"Here, you take," he said handing me the watch. "Vietnamese, they steal." With a slight bow he turned and reassumed his place in the line of march.

That act brought home all too well the differences between the native populations of Vietnam. The Montagnards were a peaceful, honest people that had for years been mistreated by Vietnamese from both north and south. They had cause not to trust the Vietnamese, and often Americans were given cause for distrusting the Vietnamese as well. Many South Vietnamese soldiers and civilians alike had no loyalty to either side in the war. In the towns Vietnamese business men would as soon screw an American in a deal, as would the prostitutes who plied their trade there. Teenage, and sometimes younger, Vietnamese boys would accost GIs on the street offering them drugs, pornography and, when those were rejected, their "virgin" sisters. I have never figured out if such hunger for the almighty dollar was in their nature, or if they were perverted by the insatiable appetite of the American GI. In either case, there was a vast moral gulf between Vietnamese, and Montagnards.

Our two in one mission didn't last much longer. The command structure at Mary Lou moved with amazing alacrity. By mid afternoon they had established a permanent relay site on a hilltop firebase for 155 millimeter Howitzers. Two Romeo, the site's call sign, would nearly double the range of our teams.

In the late afternoon we were extracted, and returned to Mary Lou. After I got cleaned up I headed for the Bunker Bar to unwind, and, I hoped, find out about Matty's contact. I was in luck, Matty himself was ensconced behind the bar, and the usual suspects, including Barrio, Neugard, and Torres were occupying the stools. I took the last unoccupied stool at the end of the bar.

"Give me a bourbon," I said. "Then you can tell me what happened on that mountain you were on."

"Hell, that will take to long, he'll get all serious, and start to stutter." Barrio said, gently kidding his friend about his speech impairment. "I've already heard it, and can tell a shorter version."

"It's true," Matty said, handing me my drink. "When I'm being a smart ass I don't stutter at all, but when I ta-ta-try to be serious it's Ka-Katy bar the door."

"Okay," I said, "Barrio you tell it, but Matty, if he screws it up, feel free to jump in."

"Here they are," Barrio said, "Matty and his team, sitting on top of this hill not worrying about anything, but having to transmit messages back to Seven Niner Charlie at BTOC. Then all at once the North Vietnamese decides they want the hill that he is on. So, all at once Matty and his guys are surrounded by about two companies of NVA, and things start to get hot.

"Matty and his guys are cooped up in this old bunker on top their hill, shooting out all sides. They repulse the first attack with Claymores, grenades, and automatic rifles. Matty calls for gunships, but the gooks attack again before the gunships get there. Well, the Lerps make it hot for the NVA again, and drive them back. This time, though one of Matty's guys sees one of the bad guys go down, but he rolls down the hill a ways, where you can't see the body.

"Well, Matty reports it to Seven Niner Charlie, and all at once Seven Niner grabs the horn, himself."

"The Major, himself?" I said.

"Yeah, Roger that," Barrio said. "Anyhow, the Major grabs the horn, and he says to Matty, 'Two Charlie, this is Seven-Niner, I've got a grudge to settle, go down and get me that body.'"

"He has a grudge to settle?" Neugard asked incredulously.

"Yeah, that's what he said. Now Matty thinks a bit, there's two hundred of them and only four of our guys, this does not seem like a good time to leave the bunker, and go looking for the body of a guy that may have rolled all the way down to where his buddies were waiting. So Matty tells the Major, 'Seven-Niner,' he says clear as a bell, 'I've got a life to live, there's no way I'm going after that body!'"

"I was being a smart ass," Matty said.

"Next, Matty is asking the Major to extract him, but the Major says that their mission as radio relay is to valuable, and they will have to tough it out."

"No shit?" Torres said.

"No shit," Barrio said. "But at least by now the gun ships were on station, and blasting away at the bad guys with rockets and miniguns. Now, Matty is noting that these gunships are Charlie Models,[1] not Cobras. So he gets on the horn to the gunship pilot and says, 'wha-wha-why don't you gu-gu-guys ka—come down here and pi-pi—pick us up?'

"Now, the gunship pilot says, 'I would like to do that, but we can not do it unless it is a Tac-E.'

"What's a Tac-E?" I asked.

"That is exactly what Matty wants to know. 'Ta-ta-Tac-E,' Matty says. 'Wh-what's a Tac-E?'

"'A Tac-E is a tactical emergency,' the pilot tells him. 'That means that if we don't pick you up, you are going to get your asses shot off.'

"'Ta-ta Tac-E, Ta-ta Tac-E,' Matty shouts, and so hearing the magic words, the pilot comes down and picks them up."

"I guess you've just got to know what to say," I said.

"Amen, ba—brother," Matty said.

---

1. The Charlie Model gunships were converted Hueys and had the capacity to carry passengers, whereas the Cobras were narrow and did not have a passenger compartment.

20

The LRP That Cried Wolf

Thursday February 27, 1969

Dear Diary,

Just back from talking with Massoletti. We're going out in the morning and a reporter is going with us ...

Plaskett and I liked to know what was going on. On the third day in camp after a mission the Team Leader would receive a visual reconnaissance of the Teams next AO and would then go to S-2, where Major McIntosh, more commonly known as Seven Niner, would brief him on the mission. Plaskett and I would watch for Massoletti's return, and show up at his tent to find out what we would be up against.

"Frost has been assigned as ATL for this mission," he said on this particular day. Frost was an unknown quantity. He was a friendly enough guy, but a bit of a braggart. Like most guys he bragged about the women he had slept with, but, unlike most, his proudest claim to fame was the amount of pot he had consumed. He often said that he had smoked so much pot that he could go a week without it, and all he needed to do was take a deep breath, and he would go under again.

"There will be five of us on this mission," Massoletti said and then paused. A five man team was not that unusual, though because of manpower shortages they were becoming rarer. Plaskett and I waited to find out which LRP was going to join us. "They're sending a reporter out with us," he said finally.

"A civilian?" Plaskett asked.

"Yeah, some sort of a free lancer, named Roberts. He gets a lot of his stuff published in the Detroit Free Press. Now he's doing a story on Rangers."

"I haven't seen any of them," I said. "We're still pretty much Lerps around here."

Massoletti grinned. "Officially—they are us. We'll have to do 'till something better comes along."

"Damn," I said, "we've been doing the job for nearly three years, and nobody's ever heard of us and within a month of them changing us to Rangers, all at once they've got reporters hanging around."

"I heard about one story in some men's magazine," Plaskett said.

"Nobody reads men's magazines," I said. "They just look at the pictures."

My first impression of Roberts was a good one. He was rather impressive, tall, and well built. We soon found out that he would have passed muster as a LRP. He was, also a genuine nice guy. It appeared that this would be a more pleasant mission than we expected. He was good company, and I figured that the brass wouldn't dare send us out with a reporter if the AO we were going into was anywhere near the bad guys.

In fact the AO was down right beautiful. It seemed to be a microcosm of the Central Highlands packed into four grid squares. It was mostly jungle, as would be expected in the Central Highlands, but there was a nice little river that ran through it, and just enough grass land to provide ample LZs, and mimic the geographic contrasts of the region as a whole.

Massoletti, Plaskett and I treated it as a normal mission, at least at first. It was basically a training mission for Roberts. He could learn by example what went on during a typical LRP mission. From the first, however, Frost seemed to be trying to create a story. Not long into his watch on the very first night out he shook us awake.

"Movement," he said in a horse whisper.

We sat on alert, waiting and watching. The minutes passed slowly. No abnormal sounds emanated from the jungle. No voices, no snapping of twigs, no clanking of metal equipment, only the normal sounds of the night time jungle. Finally, maybe a half hour later, Massoletti was convinced there was no danger.

"False alarm," he whispered, "go back to sleep."

In the morning when we were bringing in our Claymores Frost scurried back with his Claymore. "Look what I found," he said holding out a cheap pocket knife, like the ones sold in the bazaars in every Vietnamese town. "I think they were trying to cut the wires to our Claymores."

"Why would they do that?" Roberts asked.

"So they could rush us!" Frost said.

"Hum," Massoletti said. "I wonder why they would cut the wires, when all they would have to do was turn the Claymore around to where it was facing us? Then, when they started shooting we would blow ourselves up."

Frost said no more.

On the third day out that we came upon a beautiful little creek in the middle of a small field. It meandered its way from the jungle beyond, forced itself between boulders, then gushed forth into a shimmering pool. It was a hot day. We were dirty, we were sweaty, and the pool was cold, and the force of the little waterfall could scrub the dirt and fatigue from our bodies.

Frost was first to suggest that we take a swim. Massoletti hesitated. It went against his better judgement, but there was a siren in that pool with a song as seductive as that of any Lorelei. He lay down his CAR-15, stripped off his clothes, and dove in. Frost and Roberts were not far behind.

Plaskett hesitated a little longer then began removing his clothes. He looked at me, I had made no move to remove my clothes. "Aren't you going in?" he asked.

"Somebody has to stand guard," I said.

"Ok," he said, and jumped into the pool.

They swam and played like children for fifteen, or twenty minutes while I kept my eyes peeled on the tree line, stealing only an occasional peek at the cool, and inviting water. Plaskett finally took pity on me, and swam back to where I stood watch.

"Go on in," he said. "I'll take over."

I hesitated, not because I didn't want to go in, but because I remembered how safe I felt on that training mission when all at once bullets began to fly. I didn't want to be that far from my rifle. But the sirens song of the pool was too strong, I dropped my Swedish K into the pile of rifles stripped off my gear and clothes, and jumped in.

I know something about creeks, I grew up around them, and have swum in many an isolated pool, but never was there such a creek as this, never was the water colder or clearer, and never a waterfall that could massage tired muscles so well. I don't know what heaven is like, but I would imagine that God would put creeks like this one there.

I might have remained forever, but Massoletti was more easily sated by the Lorelei of the creek. When he climbed out and began to dress it was a signal for the rest of us to follow suit. We donned our gear, and turned our footsteps back to the jungle. In myth the siren lured sailors to their death with her song. We had escaped the pleasant song of the rushing water. Had we tarried longer, perhaps our fate would have been the same as those ancient sailors.

The river that ran through the AO was fat and lazy compared to our creek. Along the river bank in a patch of jungle we found a natural bowl in the earth. It was an ideal night location. A large field opened up a few yards away providing us with a handy LZ.

We set up our camp, put out our Claymores, and settled in for our last night in the field. After we ate our rations we talked in whispers until dark. Frost dominated the talk, trying to impress Roberts with the gore, and danger that confronted him specifically, on a daily basis. He told Roberts what he would do if he were Team Leader, about how he would have found a trail that he would follow until he found who ever it was that had tried to disable our Claymores. I could tell that Massoletti was annoyed, to tell the truth I was too. Finally, Massoletti put a stop to his bragging by assigning him second watch, and reminding him that he had better get some sleep before it was his time to assume that duty.

We wouldn't move the next day. We had a perfectly good LZ right by us, and despite Frost's hype, there didn't seem to be anything else to learn from this AO. We would wait in our night location until the helicopters came to pick us up.

Fog blanketed the river when we awoke. It was, evidently, more wide spread than just our AO. We learned from Seven Niner Charley that the helicopters couldn't fly out of Mary Lou until it burned off. The estimated time for our extraction was put back from 900 hundred hours until 1100 hours. At eleven, it was again set back until afternoon. The fog had burned off by ten o'clock, but it had caused a backlog in the flight schedule.

As we now had time to kill we decided to entertain our guest. Massoletti and I treated Roberts to a knife throwing demonstration. Massoletti was pretty good with the large bowie knife he carried, but my commando knife still managed to eke out a narrow victory. Plaskett suggested we show Roberts how to fish with a fragmentation grenade. As the explosion would be under water, and would not make a great noise, Massoletti gave his approval. The grenade was tossed into the water followed in a few seconds with a hollow 'whoom.' Shortly, to the amusement of all, the unconscious carcasses of three or four large dog fish floated to the surface.

Frost, evidently over his apprehension about knife wielding Vietcong, suggested that we demonstrate the power of a Claymore mine. He suggested we use one of our mines to blow down the lone tree that strayed into our LZ. .

"No, that would make too much noise," Massoletti said. "Besides the tree is far enough off that it wouldn't keep the helicopter from landing."

"Come on man," Frost argued, "Roberts needs to know the power we could throw at the enemy if we were attacked."

"And blowing a Claymore would give any enemy within miles our exact location." Massoletti responded.

"Well, what if we did it when we knew the birds were on the way?"

Massoletti thought for a moment. "Yeah, that would be ok," he said.

At around 12:30 Massoletti called Seven Niner Charlie to see if the birds were in the air. He was told that they were. We set a Claymore against the tree and strung out the electric wire. I argued that we should use the front blast so that all 700 ball bearings in the mine would be driven into the tree, but Frost thought that the back blast was strong enough to do the job. As it was his show, I let him have his way. He attached the charging handle, snapped back the safety and crunched down on the handle.

The blast was loud and impressive, but not so impressive as the root structure of that tree. The tree shook violently but remained erect.

"One more time," Frost said. "That tree couldn't stand another blast like that."

"No," Massoletti said emphatically. "We're not going to waste another Claymore."

As soon as he had put his foot down, Seven Niner Charlie's voice could be heard calling us on the radio. "Two Echo, Two Echo, Seven-Niner Charlie, over."

Massoletti picked up the handset. "Roger, Seven-Niner Charlie, this is Two Echo, over."

With the handset against Massoletti's ear, we could no longer hear Seven Niner Charlie's end of the conversation, but the expression on Massoletti's face told us that he didn't like what he was hearing. "Roger, out," he said finally.

"The birds are in the air," he told us, "but they won't be picking us up until sixteen hundred hours. It seems that they have to deliver some brass to Pleiku before they come our way."

We had announced our location to the world and would now have to wait another three and a half hour to be picked up. "No more wasting munitions," the Team Leader said, "we may need them yet."

We pulled back into our night location, behind the defensive perimeter of our remaining three Claymores, and waited. We would have time enough to pull in the Claymores, and pack them away when the helicopters were truly on the way. We still believed it was a safe AO, that there weren't any NVA or VC for miles. After all we had been there for four days and hadn't seen or heard any sign of them, unless, of course, we were to believe Frost's story about the knife he said he had found. Still, we weren't going to take any more unnecessary chances.

Time moved ponderously that afternoon. The sweep second hand on my watch seemed to creep along in its circuit from twelve to twelve. We didn't talk much, we just watched and listened. We neither saw nor heard anything unusual. The birds sang, leaves rustled in the gentle breeze, Roberts' pen scratched across the pages of his notebook, and the river lapped against the shore. Otherwise, all was quiet.

Finally, about a half hour before we had been told they would be there, the radio crackled with the news that the helicopters were on their way. We pulled in the Claymores and packed them away, swung the packs onto our backs, and headed into the LZ. Soon we could hear the rotors. We marked our location with yellow smoke. The helicopter pilot identified the color. The extraction craft came down the river, popped over the little patch of jungle, and landed softly in the LZ. We boarded on both sides, Massoletti, Robert's and Frost from one side and Plaskett and I from the other. As the bird lifted off Frost looked out toward the jungle on the other side of the LZ.

"My God," he said, "There's NVA over there. Maybe a dozen of them."

Here we go again, I thought, is he ever going to stop crying wolf. Massoletti leaned forward where he too could see what Frost was looking at.

"Oh, shit," he said.

Now I looked too. I didn't see any NVA, but I did see what Massoletti saw, the contrail of an enemy B-40 rocket as it streaked not ten feet below the helicopter. So much for a safe AO.

21

Lookout

Saturday March 8, 1969

Dear Diary,

We're going to a place called Poli Kleng; we're going to be perched on top a mountain ...

The infantrymen who had to climb it called it Kickass Mountain. Like other mountains given the same, or similar names by GIs, it was tall and steep. I don't know how long we had sat on top of that mountain, a week for sure, maybe longer. Our mission was to sit on top of Kickass, and watch for rocket attacks on LZ Bass, a firebase near the remnants of a village called Polei Kleng. The fire base lay in a plain beyond the base of the mountain, four or five klicks to the northwest. There had been four of us to start, but one of the team had gotten sick, and had to be extracted. Now we were down to three, Massoletti, Plaskett and me.

It was an easy mission, no humping, the chopper dropped you on top of the mountain, and there you stayed. We ate C-Rations cooked over a C-4 fire instead of LRP Rations, and whenever we ran low we ordered more, and the choppers delivered it. They even brought us our mail. It was a pretty good life except for the fact that we were sitting pretty much on a bald mountain top with very few places to hide. The GIs that had given the mountain its moniker had cleared the trees from the top, to give themselves a field of fire. I guess that was fine if there were a couple of hundred of you, and you had listening posts set up on all sides of the mountain. But, there were only three of us up here now, and we were three guys that were used to having trees to hide behind. Here there was nothing to hide behind except for a couple of sandbag lined pits that were the remnants of bunkers built by the line units. From our vantage point on top of the mountain we could see for many miles in all directions, but because of the steepness of the slope, we couldn't see the jungle a hundred meters away.

We did, of course, take precautions. We had our personal armaments, Massoletti's CAR-15, Plaskett's M-16, and my Swedish K, and M-79. In addition we had brought extra fragmentation and white phosphorus grenades. Before we had left Mary Lou, Massoletti has laid out some "Delta Juliets." That was what we called our pre-plotted artillery targets. Every other unit in Vietnam seemed to call these "Delta Tangos." Why the Second Brigade called them called them "Delta Juliets" and what the "J" in Juliet stood for remains a mystery to me. We had, also set out three or four Claymores around our perimeter.

To give us early warning of trouble Massoletti sent Plaskett down to the edge of the clearing to set out some trip flares. He didn't tell us where they were, but, as we had no intention of leaving the top of the hill, it didn't seem to matter. What mattered was, that if the bad guys chose to pay us a visit, we would have sufficient warning of their arrival to prepare a welcome for them.

But, as I said before, it was an easy mission. We had been there over a week, and had had no trouble. It looked like we were going to take back everything we had brought with us.

The view from the mountain was spectacular. To the northwest we looked down on LZ Bass. With the naked eye you could see the helicopter pad, and the command bunker, and with the help of binoculars you could make out the tents and the battery of 155 mm self-propelled Howitzers. To the northeast and east was the jungle covered ridge that was the primary focus of our attention. Below the ridge, and winding through the jungle around our mountain was the road that led from Kontum to Polei Kleng. To the west and southwest a broad valley trailed off toward the horizon.

It was through that valley one day, that we saw an invisible giant walk. At least that's how it appeared. We were watching an Arclight, the code name for a B-52 strike. You could not see or hear the plane, but you saw the bomb craters appear from nowhere, as if they were the giant's footprints, and the distant rumbling of the exploding bombs were like the thudding of heavy, unseen boots upon the ground.

As interesting a diversion as an Arclight was, it was still a diversion. Our mission was to watch the hills to the east, and southeast, to see if we could spot where the North Vietnamese were launching the 122 mm rockets that had been harassing LZ Bass. The NVA were not being very cooperative, however, they seemed to have taken a respite from their attack. Not once during our time on Kickass did they launch a rocket. Soon, we would find that they had something else up their sleeves.

It was mid morning, we looked up from our game of Casino, and saw the line of tracks snaked their way down the road that led to LZ Bass. There were two tanks, one on either end of the convoy, with ten or twelve Armored Personnel Carriers strung out between them. They stretched for nearly two kilometers.

"I wonder what unit that is?" I asked.

"I think the Second of the Eights is at LZ Bass," Massoletti said. "We haven't seen anybody leave so it's not a platoon returning from a mission. They might be reinforcements."

The lead tank had just reached the big bend in the road, just before it straightened out for the last run to LZ Bass, when, suddenly the ground all around the tracks began to erupt with big, and small geysers of dirt. Fire erupted all along the entire line, emanating from the jungle that lay between our mountain, and the road. The NVA had launched an ambush on the tracks. After a few seconds delay, the rattling of small arms fire, and the explosions of B-40 rockets reached our ear. The lead APCs received a direct hit from a B-40, and was knocked out of action, the others maneuvered to reduce their profile, and brought their machine guns into action. There must have been at least two companies of North Vietnamese to enfilade the entire column. It was a full fledged battle, and we were in the catbirds seat.

Of all the LRPs that I have known I don't know of any two that were more in sync during contact than Massoletti, and I. Massoletti grabbed the radio's handset, reported the contact and got transferred to the firebase at LZ Bass. Meanwhile, I had anticipated his need, and located the middle of the NVA line on the map, plotted the coordinates, and was encrypting them. Then, I read out the encoded message, Massoletti repeated it to the battery, and within a couple of minutes of the onset of the attack a 155 millimeter smoke round landed in the middle of the enemy.

"Repeat H E," Massoletti ordered, and the first high explosive round exploded amidst the smoke of the marker round. "Give me a battery!" and 155s began exploding all along the NVA line.

And, of all the LRPs that I have known, I don't know of any more anxious to get into a fight than Plaskett. "I'm going to try to get closer, to see if I can help," he told us and ran down the ridgeline to where it dropped off sharply in an effort to get nearest to the fight. Now, with my map reading and coding duties done, and the fine adjustments in the artillery fire in Massoletti's capable hands, I too was left with nothing to contribute to the fight. Besides, I could see that Plaskett was not going to do any good from this range with an M-16, but perhaps, with the steepness of the mountain, my M-79 might have some effect. I grabbed the grenade launcher, and headed after Plaskett. I could see him at the end of the ridge, and except for some stubble of brush, the trail was quite clear. Plaskett saw me coming and turned.

"Look out for the …"

Suddenly it was the forth of July, with fireworks shooting straight up into the sky.

"… trip flare," he shouted belatedly.

I beat on the thing with the butt of my '79, and though I couldn't put it out, I at least got it pointed toward the ground. "Well if they didn't know we were here before, they certainly do now," I thought. There was nothing that could be done about it now. I joined Plaskett and fired a couple of rounds in the direction of the battle. I quickly learned the futility of trying to get an M-79 round to travel three kilometers. Even though the mountain was steep it was still not a cliff. It seemed to be a wasted, and counter productive effort. It wasn't. It woke us to a problem much closer at hand.

A rifle bullet travels at some 1,700 feet per second, much too fast for the human eye to follow, at least in most instances. But, when you are in the middle of battle, and the adrenaline is pumping, you can do, and see amazing things. I heard the popping of small arms fire from below us, and I saw the bullets flying over our heads. The enemy was in the jungle just below us. For some time I blamed myself for attracting them when I set off the trip flare, but with the clarity of time I realized that they could not have covered that much distance and climbing such a steep hill, in the couple of minutes that had elapsed since my blunder. They had been there all the time, and had probably planned an attack on us in coordination with the ambush of the tracks.

"Let's get out of here," I told Plaskett.

"You go on, I'll cover the retreat," he said.

"How are you going to cover us with that thing," I said pointing to his M-16. "It can't fire over the edge of the hill, but this can." I held up the M-79. "Now get out of here and let me do my job."

I backed up the hill, dropping '79 rounds over the crest as quickly as I could load and fire. Massoletti met us at the top of the hill, and deployed us along the upper crest. Gun ships were now on station at the site of the ambush, relieving him of the responsibility of directing artillery fire. He had already reported that we, too, were under enemy attack.

I tried using the Swedish K, holding it over my head and firing over the crest, but I soon realized I was accomplishing nothing more than making noise. For the time being we were making the only noise, the enemy had ceased firing. We had to presume that they were maneuvering to come at us from a different direction. I returned to using the '79, popping rounds in a fan shape down the hill. I hadn't fired more than five or six rounds when all hell broke loose. I had evidently found a soft spot.

"Don't we have a Delta Juliet down there?" I asked Massoletti.

"Roger that." He grabbed the handset. "Red Badge Alpha, this is Two Echo, fire Delta Juliet two—zero-zero-two, give me smoke, over," We saw a puff of smoke from a single gun on LZ Bass. Before the shot even hit he was barking out his next order.

"Repeat H—E!"

And again while the shot was still in the air …

"Give me a battery!"

The hill below us was inundated by a storm of explosions, with counterpoint provided by the crashing of trees struck by 155 millimeter projectiles. When the artillery had done all the damage that they could, the gunships, now finished at the ambush site, took a turn. Down below the remnants of the line of tracks moved on toward the relative safety of LZ Bass. Before too long the helicopters ran out of targets of opportunity. The enemy was in retreat—all was quiet. The gunships peeled off and returned to their base.

Now, only the three of us were left on the hill, waiting and listening. In due time we heard what we were listening for, the flip, flip, flip of the rotors of the Slick that was coming to take us home.

22

A Bronze Star for Massoletti

Tuesday March 18, 1969

Dear Diary,

I've thought about leading my own team. I think I could be a good Team Leader. I've run missions with some of the best. But I'd never told anybody about it …

"You should be a ta-team leader," Mateer said, pushing a plastic cup of bourbon across the bar to me. It was the day after we got off of Kickass Mountain, and we were the only two in the Bunker Bar. "After all you're probably the smartest guy in this ou-outfit."

I took a sip. "I don't know Matty," I said, "I want to have my own team, but the officers don't seem to feel the same way you do. Hell, they only made me an assistant team leader once, and that was on a team where I was the only American besides the team leader, the other two team members were Montagnards."

"The officers doe—don't know shit. They said they needed team leaders, and asked me who I thought should be wa-one. I toe-toe-told them that you should. It doesn't mean that they'll ta-take my advice, ba-but I told th-them what I thought."

"I appreciate it Matty, but they haven't made anyone a team leader that wasn't a Sergeant since Finley was lost."

"Rank da-doesn't mean anything," he said.

"Maybe not to us, but it seems to mean something to the brass. If you notice the board up in the HQ tent, where they have Finley marked as MIA, he's now a Sergeant."

"That's a hell of a way to make rank," Matty, the smart ass, said without the hint of a stutter. "Honest, ma-man," he said getting serious again. "You need to ask them to make you a ta-team leader."

"They're supposed to be the leaders," I said. "They should be seeking out the best people, and offering them the position. I've always thought that you should be recognized for your talents, you shouldn't have to foist yourself on others to get what you want."

"That ain't the way the world acts, my friend. You ga-got to ask for something before they'll give it to you."

"You may be right," I said. "Maybe I'll finish my tour as a damn good rear security, that never went any farther."

Plaskett stuck his head in the door. "Hey, Reed," he said. "Massoletti just came back from BTOC, and want's to see us in his tent."

"Okay," I said. "I'll be right there." I tossed the empty cup in the trash, and turned back to Mateer. "Thanks, Matty, it's nice to know that somebody recognizes your abilities."

"Think na-nothing of it man," he said as I went out the door.

Massoletti was sitting on his bunk, and Plaskett was sitting on the bunk across from his. I sat down next to Plaskett. "What's up Tango Lima?" I asked.

"Well," Massoletti said looking down at the floor, "we must have done something right up on that hill. We evidently played hell with the North Vietnamese's plans. We broke up their ambush real good. The Major is proud of what we've done." He looked up at us.

"They're going to give me a Bronze Star with V for valor," he said. "I told them it was a team effort and that you guys should get one too, but they didn't see it that way. I then said that, maybe they could give you Army Commendation Medals with Vs. But they wouldn't go for that either."

"It's nice to know you thought of us," I said. "But, if the brass think it was only a one medal contact, there's nothing we can do about it. You're the one that deserves it, you were the guy in charge."

"Yeah, I agree," Plaskett said. "Besides, If we're lucky we may get another chance at a medal."

"Oh, yeah," I said, "and, if we're unlucky we may have several."

They held the ceremony to award Massoletti his Bronze Star in the tent that they used for a chapel. It was on top the hill between the mess hall and the officers tents. Two rows of benches were separated by a central aisle. The religious paraphernalia was moved aside, and officers sat on the dais. There was a General among them. I don't know who he was, my seat was too far away to read the name on his fatigues. I don't remember the names of many officers, especially those above the rank of Captain. If they didn't deal with LRPs on a daily basis, I guess I didn't see any reason to learn their names. I only knew of two of the Generals that were then in Vietnam, General Abrams, who had replaced Westmoreland as overall commander, and General Pepke, who commanded the Forth Division. I know this one wasn't Abrams, but it might have been Pepke. The Colonel commanding the Second Brigade was there too, as was Major McIntosh, the Intelligence Officer, and Captain Connerville.

Captain Connerville officiated. He rose, and took his place behind a lectern at the corner of the dais. "Sergeant Larry L. Massoletti," he announced. Massoletti marched down the center aisle and stood at attention in front of the dais. He was dressed in his best Tigers, and a new LRP hat. The General rose and stood in front of Massoletti.

"Sergeant Massoletti is awarded a Bronze Star with V device," Connerville read from a sheet of paper in front of him, "for heroism in connection with military operations against an armed hostile force in the Republic of Vietnam...." He recounted the contact from the award certificate emphasizing Massoletti's coolness under fire. Fortunately the citation neglected to mention my clumsiness in setting off a trip flare and revealing our location to the enemy. "Sergeant Massoletti's exceptional courage, initiative, and exemplary devotion to duty are in keeping with the highest traditions of the military service, and reflect great credit upon himself, his unit, and the United States Army." Connerville read.

The General stepped down from the dais, and pinned the medal on Massoletti's chest. He stepped back, Massoletti saluted, and the General returned the salute. Then, Massoletti did an about face, and marched back to his seat in the rear of the tent.

They repeated the ceremony for another GI who had, also done something good but, as I didn't know him, I wasn't paying much attention. When we were dismissed I got out of the flow of traffic as soon as I could, and lit a cigarette. Plaskett came up to me.

"Wow," he said, "that was quite a ceremony. To think we could have been up there too. I wonder why they didn't think it was worth more than one medal?"

"Maybe the General only had time to hand out one medals today," I said taking a deep drag, "or maybe they think my setting off the trip flare drew the enemy to our location."

"You think so? They couldn't have got up that mountain that quick."

"Then, I guess the General didn't have enough time."

We walked back to the LRP area in silence. Plaskett went back to his tent, and I wandered into the Headquarters tent. Shaner was the only one there. He looked up when I entered.

"Hey, Reed, what's up?" he said.

"You missed a neat ceremony," I said. "They gave Massoletti a Bronze Star."

"I guess I've seen too many ceremonies. Somebody had to watch things down here, so I said I would. I hear you guys had quite a time up there on that mountain."

"Yeah, it got hot for a while, but we came out without a scratch."

"Not exactly," he said lighting a cigarette.

"What do you mean?"

"I found out that we did have a loss in that contact. He wasn't a Lerp anymore, but he'd been one of us."

I looked at him quizzically. "Who?"

"Sergeant Blake was in command of an APC that was hit by a B-40 in that contact. He was killed instantly."

"Damn," I said. "I had no idea."

"There was no way you could know. When everybody is locked up in those boxes you can't see who's who, especially not from three or four klicks away." He took a long drag off of his cigarette. "I got another piece of news for you."

"Better, I hope."

"No, I don't think so. You remember a guy who came in with you, named Murphy?"

"Yeah, he was my best buddy when he was here. Has something happened to him, too?"

"He's missing in action, and presumed dead," Shaner said. "I hate to be the one to give you the bad news."

"That's ok," I said. "Bad news doesn't seem to hurt so much anymore. After a while you just get numb. What is it about war? You meet a guy, and you really like him, instantly he becomes a good buddy, and his name is Finley, and all at once he's gone, and it hurts bad. And you have another good buddy and his name is Hancock, and then he's gone and it still hurts, but you get over it quicker. Then, you find out the guy who brought you to the platoon has been killed, and you've seen it happen—and you shrug it off. Then, another guy who was your best friend is killed, and the feelings that should be there—just aren't."

"I know what you mean, man," Shaner said. "You build up defenses. Before long you stop making friends out of fear you will lose them. You meet guys, and drink with them, and laugh and have a good time, but the next day when you see them you have to look at the name on their fatigue pocket to know who they are."

"Shaner, that's starting to happen to me."

"Let it happen, man. It's the only way you can keep from going nuts."

23

The Ones That Got Away

Friday March 28, 1969

Dear Diary,

So much has been going on here. With Massoletti's award ceremony and the news about Murphy and Blake, I guess I should have wanted time to get my feelings straight. If I had any feelings left, that is. But we're going out again, I don't have time to think about it ...

I guess the first sign that it was going to be a tough mission, was the chattering of the machine gun as we ran toward the tree line. I didn't know why he was shooting, it had been a clean insertion. The insertion slick had dropped down onto the grassy hillside that was our L Z, and the chase ship had passed over the top. There was only a brief interlude when a watcher would not have had seen four helicopters in the air. We were off the bird in a flash, and headed toward the tree line. Everything was just like normal. Then the door gunner opened up.

What was he shooting at? Did he see the enemy? There was no answering fire, no sign of movement in our front. It wasn't a long burst, just a short rattle, maybe twenty rounds, but one round would have been long enough to destroy the stealth of the insertion.

"What was that all about?" I asked Massoletti as we settled into a defensive position just inside the tree line.

"I don't know," he said with a look of disgust on his face. "Maybe he was just taking target practice."

We sat there for about an hour, just to make sure that no bad guy had come around to investigate the firing. Then we headed off into the jungle. There were four of us, Massoletti as usual walked his own point and carried the radio. Plaskett was next in line, assigned to keeping his eye on the left flank. A LRP called by the nickname of Chug-a-lug walked third, watching things on the right, and I, as usual, brought up the rear, making sure we weren't being followed, and covering our trail as best I could.

Even though we hadn't been there before, we knew the territory. It had been two weeks since Massoletti, Plaskett, and I had been sitting on top of Kickass Mountain on the other side of the valley. This was the section of jungle that we had been watching for signs of the rockets the NVA were firing at LZ Bass. Ironically, after we were extracted, the team Chug-a-lug was on got put on Kickass, and had their own encounter with the bad guys.

Our objective on this mission was the same, to find the enemy that was firing on LZ Bass, but the tactic had changed. Now, instead of watching the hills from the vantage point of the tallest mountain, we were to do the job on the ground, to go into the crucible, to find the enemy, and to destroy him.

We kept moving until late afternoon, then pulled twenty or thirty yards off the trail, and set up our night location. We didn't tempt fate by heating our LRP rations, the smell would carry too far, we ate them cold instead. We shot the bull in low whispers until dark, then Massoletti established the guard rotation, and we turned in for the night. Around three in the morning Chug-a-lug woke us. "We've got movement," he whispered to each of us as he gave us a gentle shake to bring us around.

In silence we reached for our weapons and pulled them close to our bodies. Four pair of highly attuned ears swept the night. Four pair of hands took their weapons off safe and made them ready to fire. Four bodies coiled to spring into action in the merest instance, and four hearts pounded just a bit faster. There are always noises in the jungle, the chirping of insects, reptiles slithering through the undergrowth or up the bark of trees, small animals scurrying to their dens, and the occasional night stalking predator seeking its prey. There are always noises, the problem is separating the normal from the threatening. Thirty, maybe forty minutes later—nothing.

"Sorry guys," Massoletti finally said, "go back to sleep."

We didn't move out until mid-morning. It's best to stay in your night location for the first two, or three hours of sun light, because that's when the bad guys are prone to be on the move. If your night location is close to a trail they may pass in front of you without seeing you, allowing you to call in artillery without being discovered. But, they didn't pass by us that morning. Around 9:30 or 10:00 we got ready to take to the trail. It was while we were packing that I realized that I had lost my British Commando knife. I always carried it strapped horizontally across the back of my web belt. It was the last of the half dozen that my brother had sent me. I'd given four of them away, and kept two for myself. I'd lost one earlier, and now had lost the second one.

We explored until about noon when we pulled off the trail once again to eat our lunch, and listen. So much of what we did involved listening. In the jungle you could hear a lot farther than you could see. Unmuffled voices, a cough, the clanking of equipment, or the snapping of a twig could warn you of danger long before your eyes confirmed the presence of the enemy. When I left Vietnam the army would test my hearing before discharging me, they found that it substantially more acute than when I enlisted.

About an hour later we were on the trail again. It wasn't long before the trail entered a narrow valley, and wound down toward the valley's head. We hadn't traveled more than fifty, or sixty yards down the valley when Massoletti stopped, and pointed down into the valley. "Look at that," he whispered. We followed his finger with our eyes and made out, among the trees about a hundred yards ahead, the vague outline of a hut. "Let's check it out," Massoletti said.

Chug-a-lug turned, and looked at me as if to say "is he crazy, why does he want to go down there?" I just shrugged my shoulders. Chug-a-lug didn't know Massoletti. Massoletti saw the job that had to be done, and didn't hesitate. Our job was to gain intelligence on the enemy, and that intelligence lay in the valley, and, maybe, in that hut.

We walked deeper into that valley. We were surrounded by triple canopy jungle, so thick that you couldn't see the sky. As we got closer we began to make out details of the hut. It was a made of grass and bamboo, about six feet wide, just as long as it was wide, and no more than five feet high. As we neared the hut we could see deeper into the valley, what we saw caused us all to hesitate simultaneously. I felt a shiver run down my spines. There were bunkers in the valley.

Forgetting the hut for the time being, Massoletti led us off the trail, and around the contour of the hill toward the head of the valley. There we could get a clear view of the whole complex.

"If there's anybody down there we could probably stir them up with a few artillery rounds," Massoletti whispered. He took off his pack, and switched on the radio. While he made contact with the fire base, I motioned to Plaskett, and he followed me back up the hill a few paces, where we set out Claymores to guard against any unwanted visitors from the trail. Massoletti called in the artillery, and adjusted it onto the complex. When five or six, one-five-five, high explosive rounds landing in the middle of the complex brought no response, we knew for sure that it was empty, and safe for closer exploration. We retrieved our Claymores, and moved into the bunker complex.

There were about two dozen bunkers in the complex built in two tiers along the northern slope of the hill. The grass hut, the communal area, and the kitchen were along a small creek on the floor of the valley. There was little of value in the complex, even the hut that had first drawn our attention was empty. The North Vietnamese carried everything of value with them at all times. But, the newness of the bunkers, and overall maintenance of the area showed the complex's recent habitation. The place was so fresh that the NVA might have been there just a few hours before.

At the far end of the complex we found the trail leading up the ridge on the other side of the valley. We climbed steadily up the ridge for about an hour before we reached a plateau where the ascent became more gradual. Just as we reached this level we pulled off the trail to take a rest. Between the trail and us, just where the path assumed a steeper descent, a large dead mahogany log blocked our view from the trail. On the other side of us, no more than a couple of yards from where we sat, the jungle opened up into a large field of elephant grass that swept down the opposite slope of the ridge. It was a good location from which to monitor the trail.

After an hour or so of just sitting, and watching Massoletti made a decision. "Set out some Claymores," he said. "We're going to make this our night location."

As a night location this spot had definite strengths, and one very distinct weakness. Having an open field that could serve as a LZ at our back was a strength. The log along the trail would hide us from the enemy's view until they were right on us, another strength. But our proximity to the trail, no more than 20 feet, meant that any encounter we might have with the enemy would be at point blank range, and we were almost sure to be outnumbered. This was a distinct weakness. Chug-a-lug got another of those looks on his face that indicated that he didn't like the idea, and, though I had to admit that I would have chosen a location farther off the trail, I'd been through a lot with Massoletti, and he hadn't gotten me killed yet.

But, I have to admit that I started to get the feeling that on this mission, my friend, and Tango Lima, was acting a bit differently. He wasn't taking the usual precautions to avoid contact with the enemy. He seemed in fact to be itching for a fight. As for Plaskett, I knew that he too would throw caution to the wind. If he had had his druthers, he would have set up in the bunker complex, where he would have had a sure chance to match himself against the bad guys.

We set Chug-a-lug's Claymore against the dead log aiming up the trail, and guarding the opening to our location. My Claymore was set just opposite the opening, pointing further up the trail. Its' back blast guarded the opening. Plaskett's Claymore was held in reserve.

We settled in for the night, we ate our LRP rations, we talked or we read. I'd finished the paperback I was reading so I asked to borrow one of Massoletti's "Guide Post" magazines.

"I didn't know you went in for this stuff," he said, handing me one of Norman Vincent Peal's inspirational booklets.

"You'd be surprised," I said, "Haven't you heard that there are no atheists in foxholes?" I shouldn't have been taken aback by his skepticism, after all my gambling, drinking, and trips to the whore houses in town didn't, in everyone's eyes, mark me as a child of God.

"I just never took you for the spiritual type," he said.

"When I first got in country, I had a Bible," I said. "The minister at my church gave it to me when he heard I was being sent to Nam. It had a steel plate in it. You were supposed to carry it over your heart. When I was in the hospital at Nha Trang somebody stole it. I didn't complain. I figured that he might need either the content, or the steel plate more than I did."

When it became too dark to read we turned in. Each man took his watch. Massoletti set it at one hour on, and then three hours of sleep, repeated through the hours of darkness. It was an uneventful night. My last watch began when the first streaks of dawn were painting the sky. I didn't wake my replacement when my hour was up, I called in the 'sunshine' report, and let the others sleep a bit longer. Back in the States I wasn't an early riser, but in Vietnam, especially when we were in the jungle, it seemed right. A cup of coffee would have been nice, but we were in a cold camp, and GI instant coffee didn't blend to well in unheated canteen water. Instead of having coffee, I just sat with my thoughts, and smoked.

I thought of home. I thought about Karen, my former girlfriend, that I had broken up with just before I came to Nam. I thought about my family, and, eventually I thought the thoughts that I always seemed to come back to—I thought about the war. This war was not the way I thought it would be. I heard all about the large battles of World War II, about the human wave attacks in Korea, but in this war I had been in contact four, maybe five times, and I had never seen the enemy. Well, I thought, I may have, if you count that guy in the South Vietnamese uniform, that had shot at us during the training mission. We never did find out whose side he was on. When I had been with Colbray we had shot at unseen noises coming at us it the tall grass. With Tyler and Adams, I had their word that they had ambushed enemies, that and the bullet that had ricocheted between my feet. When Neugard got nicked, I didn't see the VC that was shooting at him. On the mission with the reporter, I didn't see the bad guys, but I did see the exhaust of the rocket that they fired at us. On top of Kickass the enemy was too far away, or over the crest of the hill. I had been shot at, but never had a clear target at which to shoot back. I didn't even know if I had hurt anyone in any of these encounters. I may have caused some damage with my M-79 when I drew their fire on Kickass, but I would never know for sure.

Before too long the camp came alive, and I had to leave my contemplation. Massoletti appeared to be trying to figure out what to do next. We had found the bunker complex where the enemy had camped, we had followed, and monitored trails that were well worn by their travel, but we had not found the spots where they launched their rockets—and we had not found them. I'll never know if he made a decision, things began to happen that made his decision inevitable.

The sound that we heard wasn't a distinct sound, and it wasn't very loud. It's hard to describe, but we recognized it as the sound of heavily laden packs shifting from side to side as they are carried up a hill. Massoletti's arm reached out and pointed silently toward the trail. We turned and watched. First one, then two, then three heads appeared above the log. They looked neither left nor right, but trudged ahead under the weight of the heavy loads they carried, up the hill, past the opening, past us, and on down the trail.

I was closest to them. I swung the strap of my Swedish K over my head and stepped out onto the trail. I dropped the bolt down from its' safety position, and squeezed the trigger. Nothing—I tried again—and again nothing.

Plaskett was close beside me and saw my plight. "Use your knife!" he whispered.

Instinctively I reached behind me only to be reminded that the knife was gone. I looked down at the submachine gun, the bolt handle had not fallen into the channel that would allow the release of the bolt; it had hung up on the very edge of the safety position. By the time I dropped the bolt that last one eighth of an inch, it was too late. My quarry had disappeared around a bend in the trail.

Massoletti grabbed the handset and called in artillery trying to drive them back in our direction, but the time lapse, and our lack of knowledge of how the trailed twisted and turned doomed the attempt to failure. It was my failure, there was no doubt about it, I had had them in my sights, and they had gotten away.

24

Ambush

"We'll stay here," Massoletti said. "We've found a good hunting spot so let's use it. Those three may decide to come back, or others may be coming behind them. Put out the other Claymore and make sure, next time they don't get away."

We placed Plaskett's Claymore about 15 yards further down the trail pointed in the direction the bad guys had gone. The charging handle was placed beside the one to my Claymore. There was nothing to do now but watch and wait.

The morning drifted by, then the early afternoon. The heat of the tropical sun burned down on the jungle creating a steamy haze that hung from the trees. We had not moved the entire day, but still our clothes were damp with sweat. We didn't talk, we just listened to the jungle, the far off chattering of monkeys, the flapping of birds wings, the rustling of leaves, the buzzing of insects. Then came the snap of a twig.

I was sitting cross-legged facing the open field when I heard it. I spun around, and grabbed the two charging handles. Four pair of ears tuned toward the trail, four pair of hands clutched their weapons, and four pair of eyes watched the top edge of the log. One head—then two heads—then three heads—a fourth—and more—appeared above the log. The heads grew bodies as they ascended the hill. But, unlike before, the first head, the point man, looked left, and the point man looked right, and when he looked right he stopped, he turned. He stood staring at me sitting there, cross-legged, he stood staring at Plaskett crouching behind me. He was not more than twenty feet away, but he was, also, not more than five feet behind my Claymore, and not ten feet in front of Chug-a-lug's Claymore. All was quiet, suddenly there were no monkeys chattering in the distance, no birds flitting their wings, no rustling of leaves, or buzzing of insects, the only sound, and it seemed quite loud, was the chattering of Chug-a-lug's teeth.

The point man slowly reached up, and carefully hooked his thumb around the sling of his AK-47, and in the same motion pointed his index finger in our direction. I squeezed down hard on the charging handles. The world in front of me exploded.

The body of the point man flipped fifteen or twenty feet into the air, and came back to earth with a hollow thud. All of the heads and partial bodies that we had seen above the log, disappeared from view. They had either been blown off their feet by the Claymores back blast, or they had dived for the ground. Then came a second explosion as Chug-a-lug's Claymore delivered a coup de grace to any of the lead group that survived the first.

Now gunfire was crackling all over the place. Massoletti, cradling his Car-15 in his arms, started crawling toward the opening.

"Where are you going?" I asked.

"I'm going to get the pack off that guy," he said nodding toward the body that lay near the opening.

"Wait a minute," I said. "Let me soften them up first."

I pulled the pin on a grenade, released the handle, and let it cook off for a four count, then tossed it over the top of the log. Five—six—seven—eight seconds and then the cleansing blast of the grenade. After it exploded I raised up to a squatting position. The jungle was no longer green, nor the sky blue, all was covered by a red haze. Things did not move at normal speed, all motion was slow motion. I fired off a magazine from the Swedish K, spraying down the area as best I could. As I fired the surge of adrenaline slowly abated, so that as the last round was fired the world returned to normal color, and normal speed.

"Go for it," I said coming back down to my knees.

For a moment the enemy got very quiet, they reacted as if my Swedish K had been the M-60 machine gun that its sound mimicked, and they didn't know what they were facing. But, they were quiet only for a moment. The NVA were so close that we had no trouble hearing every non-understood syllable of an officer shouting orders to his men.

Massoletti crawled to where the point man lay. "There are three of them down out here," he yelled back at us. Then the shooting started again. A figure stepping out from behind a tree raised his AK-47 and let go a burst at Massoletti. Spurts of dust spattered his face.

Plaskett crawled down behind the log where he could see the guy who was shooting at Massoletti. The butt of his M-16 flew to his shoulder, and he unleashed a burst.

"Got him!" he yelled as the shooter wilted in his place.

Massoletti pulled back without the pack that had been so important to him only seconds before.

"That was close, that guy parted my hair," he said grinning, the ironic grin of one that had faced death and survived.

Now he went to the radio, and called in the contact. "Two Romeo, this is Two Echo, we have contact! We're in the same location as last reported. There are a lot of them. Get me artillery!" Almost as soon as said, it was done, and he had the battery at LZ Bass. He called for a marker round, but it landed so far away that we could hardly hear it. There wasn't time to direct fire from so far away.

"That's no good," he yelled into the hand set, "send us some gun ships."

Unknown to us, Massoletti's transmission was being monitored by gunships that were patrolling the area. Even before he asked for them, help was on the way.

War is a damned dangerous thing. Not only should you be concerned with the damage the enemy can do to you, but you have to realize that the same munitions that can chew up the enemy, can also bite you. As the enemy had hunkered down along the hillside out of our view, my Swedish K was no longer of much use. I grabbed my M-79 and tried to lay a few rounds on them, but the hill was too steep, the rounds flew harmlessly into the valley below. I increased the angle, still no luck—increased it again till it was nearly perpendicular. Then, wham, a H.E. round crashed into a limb above our heads. Luckily, it had not traveled far enough to arm, and fell harmlessly to earth at my feet. Chug-a-lug tried a more direct approach, he pulled the pin on a white phosphorus grenade, and threw it at the bad guy. It hit a tree and bounced back at us. All four of us hit the ground an instant before the searing shards of phosphorus went flying over our backs. They should attach one of those Surgeon General's warnings to war; "caution, munitions may be as hazardous to you as they are to the enemy."

I don't know how long we fought; the slow motion of the initial rush of adrenaline had been replaced by something that seemed to make things move faster. It didn't seem like more than five or ten minutes, before we heard the flip—flip-flip-flip of the rotors of the approaching gun ships. It was such a beautiful sound.

It was time to break off the contact. We threw grenades down the hill to keep the bad guys hugging the ground, then Plaskett and Chug-a-lug retreated into the field. Massoletti shoved a primer fuse into a bar of C-4 plastic explosive and pulled the pin. He tossed it onto the ground that we were evacuating, and then lit out to join the others. When he had gotten past me I sprayed down the area with a final blast of submachine gun fire, all the while backed my way into the tall grass of the field. By the time the slow fuse ticked off fifteen seconds, and the block of C-4 exploded, I had reached the safety of the group. We were crouched in the elephant grass, 50 or 60 yards away from the fight.

The gunships arrived, and the pilots could see us hunkered down in the grass. Massoletti was in contact with them, he had me fire an M-79 smoke round to mark where we had last seen the enemy. I dropped a round directly on top of our old night location. No sooner had the smoke burst than the pilots identified the color as yellow, and honed in on the spot. The first ship fired a salvo of rockets, then peeled off to come around for a second run. Behind him the second ship sprayed the area with minigun fire. They flew so low that we could see the faces of the pilots as they flew by.

Again and again they would fly in unleash a salvo, and peel off to be replaced by the other craft. While this was going on Massoletti got word from base camp.

"They're not going to pull us out," he said. "They're sending in an air-rifle platoon to reinforce us. We're supposed to lead them back to where the North Vietnamese are."

There is another thing about war, in battle timing is seldom perfect. In a perfect situation the gun ships would have been able to remain on station, and keep up the fire until the reinforcements arrived. That way the enemy would not be able to get back to the site, and retrieve their dead, and, of greater importance, the intelligence that those dead might carry. The timing here was far from perfect. The gun ships expended their munitions, and returned to their base, and we were left to wait in the LZ for the promised reinforcements.

Despite what their name sounds like, air-rifle platoons were not equipped with Daisy BB guns. The airmoble concept was born of Vietnam, and LRPs were an integral part of it. According to the concept, LRPs would find the enemy, and then would be supported by a rifle platoon that was on constant alert, able to be helicoptered to where ever they were needed. But, even when they are on alert, it takes some time for them to get their equipment together, travel to the helicopters, load aboard and then reach their destination. In this instance we waited for nearly an hour for the Hueys to arrive with our reinforcements.

But in time they did arrive. We watched their helicopters cruise in with no sign of the stealth of a LRP insertion. There were twice our numbers in each of the four chopper, and it took more than twice as long for each to unload. Then the choppers lumbered back into the air, and thirty two GIs ambled over to where we were. Massoletti briefed the Platoon Leader and First Sergeant, then just before we were ready to head back to the contact site, Plaskett and he came over to where I was sitting.

"Plaskett wants to walk point on the way back up there," Massoletti said, "but he wants to carry your Swedish K when he does."

"Sure," I said to Plaskett, "if you're crazy enough to walk point, you ought to have something with a bigger magazine than an M-16." I handed him the submachine gun and the leather case containing extra magazines, and took his M-16 and ammo pouches. I didn't take time to adjust the ammo belt to fit my waist but just looped it around my shoulder and across my chest.

The LRPs led the way, with Plaskett on point. When we reached the area of the contact, I looked down at the place I had so recently occupied. The foliage and blades of grass around where I had been were riddled with holes that nature had not given them.

Suddenly, Plaskett took off running. He raised the Swedish K, and let go a three shot burst, then took off running again. When we got to the top of the ridge, we saw him coming back up the hill carrying three North Vietnamese packs.

"When I got to the top of the ridge, I saw an NVA making off with these packs," he said when he got back to the top. "I fired at him but the Swedish K jammed after three shots. He dropped the packs and took off." Twice in that mission my submachine gun had displayed idiosyncrasies, first when I had been unable to remove it from safety to fire at the three NVA that had passed us, and now, for the only time while I had it, it had jammed. Strangely, in both cases the idiosyncrasy had proved to be fortuitous. In the first instance, if I had been able to shoot the three NVA we might have been extracted without having found the larger body of enemy troops. In this, the second instance, the jamming had prevented us from destroying a valuable piece of intelligence. In a metal box in one of the packs we discovered what we later learned to be the first sighting device ever captured for a 122 mm rocket. The box had three neat 9mm holes through it, but each shot had missed the delicate instrument inside. Had the gun not jammed Plaskett would have put more holes through the box, and probably would have damaged, or destroyed the site.

All of the bodies had been carried away except for one. The point man lay where he had fallen. His pack was still on his back, and his AK-47 still half slung around his arm. Through the barrel of the AK was a shiny groove, made by one of the ball bearings from Chug-a-lug's Claymore. Even so, I knew that when he was hit with the force of the second mine there had been little, if any, life left in him.

We went over that dead NVA like vultures. We seemed to want all of his gear for souvenirs. Massoletti would take home his backpack, belt and brass belt buckle. He also retrieved the picture of a young girl from the dead man. We never knew if she was the dead man's wife, daughter, or girl friend. In any case it lent humanity to that cold, dead flesh that lay in the dust of that hill side. I had dibs on the captured AK-47, but gladly gave it up, when one of the gunship pilots expressed an interest in it.

The captured packs were crammed with ledger books, and documents. We inspected them, but of course could not decipher the Vietnamese writing. Each pack contained a first aid kit, supplied by misguided Quaker pacifists in the United States. What a strange nation we are, when, in the name of peace, some of us supply Band-Aids and iodine, to ease the hurts of those who were firing deadly rockets at other Americas. The packs were repacked, and loaded aboard a helicopter which took them directly back to BTOC, at Fire Base Mary Lou.

It's not easy to look on the body of a human being that you have destroyed. The emotions are all mixed-up within you. You feel both shame and pride; shame that you've taken a human life, yet pride that you have faced the ultimate life or death challenge, and have prevailed. And, as the pride of conquest begins to well up within you, it is tainted with disgust at the realization that you are taking pride in taking a human life. Ironically, the lines of a poem kept running through my head. I couldn't remember the poet then, but the words and theme only added to my conundrum.

> "'Yes, quaint and curious war is!
> You shoot a fellow down
> You'd treat if met where any bar is,
> Or help to half-a-crown."[1]

The Air-Rifle Platoon decided that they would spend the night on our battlefield. The platoon leader and first Sergeant sent out listening posts, and established a perimeter. Then the Sergeant reached into his own pack, and brought out a six pack of beer. I don't remember the brand, and It was warm, but God was it good.

Plaskett tried to console me that maybe I hadn't killed the man that, stripped of all but his uniform, and booby trapped with a grenade, was laying only a few feet from us. He said that maybe he wasn't dead until the second Claymore hit him.

"Besides," he said, "when you blew that mine you saved my life. If he had gotten to his rifle he could have killed me."

---

1. From "The Man He Killed," by Thomas Hardy.

"I tend to think that I was in his line of fire, too," I said.

Perhaps, I think now, these many years later, my fast reaction may have saved more than my own life. There was irony in Plaskett's words, he credited me with saving his life when I was really protecting my own, and, quite clearly, his own quick reactions had saved Massoletti's life. But, all this was not clear then, for the time being the internal struggle between my conscience, and my pride continued. I tossed and turned well into the night, until, through sheer exhaustion, sleep caught up with me.

25

Hotel Two Alpha

Sunday April 1, 1969

Dear Diary,

I'm not the same man I was just a few days ago. Things have changed a lot since the last time I wrote. I hope that I'm a better man, but I really don't know. All that I know is that I've changed ...

The next day we returned to Mary Lou. When we arrived we were not taken to the LRP cantonment as we usually were. Instead we were taken directly to BTOC. The officers greeted us like old friends. They said that the Brigade had never before captured so much information at one time. The contents of their point man's pack contained the records of the platoon, and of the rockets that they had launched. They helped identify the point man as the Platoon Sergeant. The Pack with the site proved to be the pack of the commanding officer. The records weren't clear, the brass told us, but it appeared that we had been up against between seventeen and thirty-two NVA regulars.

The next day Massoletti asked Plaskett, and me to come to his tent.

"You're not going to be denied your Bronze Stars this time," he said. "I've put you both in for BSVs, and no officer is going to talk them out of giving them to you this time. They're also giving me another one."

"What about Chug-a-lug?" I asked. "He was there too."

"I couldn't do it," he said. "While you and Plaskett were fighting, I had to keep him from running. As soon as bullets started flying he hunkered down on the ground shivering like a leaf, and whining that we had to get out of there. I told him to start fighting, or I'd shoot him myself. I didn't have a choice we needed every gun we had."

I'd known that Chug-a-lug was scared, but I hadn't known he had tried to run. "But he did start fighting," I said. "He fired his Claymore not long after I fired mine."

"And, after he fired it that's when he tried to run. He didn't start fighting until I threatened him, and he didn't stop shivering until after it was all over. I can't do it," he said, with a tone of moral righteousness in his voice. "If I did it would cheapen the medals that we are going to get. You guys earned yours, I think I earned one, too—he didn't."

There was no use arguing further, Massoletti had made up his mind based on what he believed was right. To change his mind would be to debase his moral values.

"It may have been too soon after his last contact," he said, a minute later. "You know he was on the team they put up on Kickass after they took us off. They tried to overrun them too. Maybe his nerves couldn't take two tough contacts so close together."

I was glad to know that he didn't hold it against Chug-a-lug. Massoletti was a good man, willing to rationalize the shortcomings of others, but hell on himself if he should violate his owns tough standards. I also found it interesting that an officer had argued against Plaskett and me getting medals for the previous contact. Massoletti didn't say who, perhaps he didn't know, but I had my suspicions.

"I'm going on R and R in a couple of days," he said. "So this was probably our last mission together, at least for a while. I just wanted to say that it's been a pleasure serving with you guys. I'll be lucky if I get any where near as good a team when I get back."

"You've more of chance of getting a better team, than we have of getting better Team Leader," Plaskett said.

"Amen," I said.

I can't prove it, and Massoletti would never admit to it, but I think Massoletti wanted a contact on that final mission that we ran together. Given the AO there was a strong chance of contact, so he may have thought of it even before we went out, but finding such a fresh bunker complex may have been all that was needed to convince him to force a contact. He took chances that he never had before. The trail we followed was well used, and invited running into the enemy at any time. The night location he chose at the top of the hill was great for ambush, but not much good for secret observation. Consciously, or subconsciously, Massoletti wanted to give Plaskett, and me another chance to win a medal. He succeeded.

We got the orders awarding us Bronze Stars for Valor a month and a half after the contact. There was no ceremony, sometime in late June, just before I took my

In-Country R and R, I wandered down to Brigade Supply, showed them the orders, and picked up my medal. The officer that had denied us a medal for the Kickass contact couldn't deny us this time, but evidently, he could see that there was no public ceremony. I have no proof of who the officer was, but Lieutenant Miller rotated out of country in April, and Lieutenant Railwood became acting Platoon Leader.

I told myself that the ceremony was no big deal, that I didn't need some General pinning a medal on my chest to validate my manhood. But sometimes, when I was alone in my tent, laying on my bunk reading, my mind would go back to Massoletti's ceremony. I would take the orders from my footlocker, and in my mind's eye I would picture another ceremony, where I was standing there flanked by Massoletti and Plaskett. When my turn came the Captain would read out the orders.

"Reed, Thomas B. Specialist Four, United States Army, is awarded the Bronze Star with 'V' Device, for heroism in connection with military operations against an armed, hostile force in the Republic of Vietnam. Specialist Four Reed distinguished himself while serving as a Long Range Reconnaissance Patrol Team Member with Headquarters and Headquarters Company, 2nd Brigade, 4th Infantry Division. On 31 March 1969, Specialist Four Reed's team encountered an enemy artillery element west of Polei Kleng. Remaining undetected for five or six hours, the team hoped that a platoon of North Vietnamese would not spot them as they waited to ambush a larger main force. When the ambush was initiated, Claymore mines were detonated, killing three of the enemy. Subsequent searching of the enemy killed, resulted in several packets containing information vital to the allied forces. During the contact, Specialist Reed provided an effective blanket of fire, enabling his team members to relocate and call in artillery and gunship support. Specialist Four Reed's courageous acts, outstanding performance and exemplary devotion to duty are in keeping with the highest traditions of the military service and reflect great credit upon himself, his unit and the United States Army."

As always seemed the case, the story on the orders was not precisely what happened, but they sounded damn good. Then I would again think, hell, I don't need any damn ceremony, and I would put the orders away, and go back to reading my book.

◆ ◆ ◆

"I want my own team," I told Sergeant Hinkle, before he had a chance to assign me to someone else's team. Ever since my talk with Matty, I had thought about my own team. My idealism was getting me nowhere, the powers that be were not going to recognize my abilities, and offer me my own team. I had to take matters into my own hand, and start the ball rolling.

"But you've never even served as Assistant Team Leader," Hinkle said.

"That's not true," I said. "I was ATL to Williams of Echo 58th when he ran a mission in the Second Brigade area."

"We've got an opening in Recondo School that we could plug you into. That's a normal first step."

"Isn't that where you run seven miles with a forty pound pack on your back?"

"Yes," Hinkle said looking a bit askance.

"The only way I'm running seven miles is with a bunch of gooks chasing me, and I wouldn't be wearing a forty pound pack, unless there was a radio in it. Hink," I said, "I've got over six months in country, and eighteen missions under my belt. I've been in six contacts, I can go through the jungle without making a sound, I know the code book, how to read a map, and how follow a compass. What are they going to teach me that I don't already know? I've only got six months left. Less time than that, if you believe Westmoreland when he said that the average Lerp's nerves were shot after twenty-five missions. I may only have seven or eight good missions left, and I want to have them leading my own team."

Hinkle sat back in his chair. "I'll see what I can do," he said.

If I had thought about it, I would have realized what a thankless task I had asked my friend to perform. All the team leaders since Finley had been Sergeants. That meant that they had all been to NCO school. On top of that most had, also been to Recondo School. Everything I knew, I learned on-the-job. I had the skills, but not the credentials. But, Hinkle was an amazing man. He had the ear, and respect of the Company Commander, the S-2 Major, and Brigade Colonel.

"Your next mission will be with Barrio," he told me the next day. "You're going to be taking out his team, Hotel Two Alpha, and he's going to evaluate you as team leader."

Two days later I went on a visual reconnaissance of the AO we were to explore. Barrio went along, and Railwood was our guide. All that he did was to tell us when we were above the AO. We viewed the area from the open door of the Huey, about a thousand feet off the ground. The pilot made several broad circles over the area.

"Where do you think we should put in?" Barrio asked above the whirring of the blades.

"Down there, in the larger LZ," I said pointing to the area. "It leads right up to the ridge line. We can keep to the high ground, cover the area and never be more than a couple of hundred yards from an LZ."

"Good thinking," Barrio said. "Where do you want to place your Delta Juliets?"

"Put one near the head of that valley," I said pointing again to a valley just below the ridge line. "There's a blue line down there, and any NVA in the area will be using it as a water source. I'd put four more, one in the middle of each grid square. That way you're never going to have to adjust more than five hundred meters to bring guns on your target."

"I never thought of that," Barrio said, "that's a good idea."

Railwood didn't seem to be paying any attention. He was wearing a headset, and was listening to the pilot. "Seen enough?" he said after the fourth circle. "If we spend anymore time here the NVA might become suspicious."

"All right," Barrio said, "let's go home."

After the fly over the next order of business was to go to BTOC to be briefed on the mission. Major McIntosh briefed us on what intelligence they had on the AO, and we reported our intended movements to him. Once that was done, we went into the next room where we gave a Spec. Five the coordinates of our Delta Juliets, which he plotted on a large map on the wall. He then gave us the call signs and radio frequencies of the artillery batteries that would be providing us with fire support. It was a process that I would follow before each of my missions as a Team Leader.

That first mission would have gone a lot easier if we had known where we were. Not only did Railwood insert us into the wrong LZ, but he even put us in a totally different AO. A Forward Air Controller helped us locate our real location on the map. Luckily, we were close enough to where we were supposed to be to still be to be on the map we had been issued.

Eventually, we did make it to the area we were supposed to explore, and we were able to discover some intelligence. We found a well hidden bunker complex. It didn't show recent signs of habitation, but was in good enough shape to be put into use by any group of NVA that happened to be passing through the area.

"That's a good piece of intelligence," Barrio said once we were safely ensconced in our night location. "If Snoopy picks up body heat in this area the

Air Force will know just where to drop some bombs." Snoopy was a specially equipped helicopter with sensors that could detect body heat.

"Snoopy is quite a piece of equipment," I said. "Maybe it will take our jobs before long."

"Not likely," Barrio said. "They sent me out one time after Snoopy had smelled a lot of activity in an area. Based on Snoopy they sent in a B-52 strike. My team was supposed to go in and count the bodies.

"When I got to the location I called S-2. Seven-Niner grabbed the horn himself, and the first thing he asked was if I had found any bodies. I said 'yes, hundreds of them.' I could almost feel the Major's excitement through the handset. I let it sink in for a minute then I said, 'I've never seen so many dead monkeys.'"

The faces of the entire team broke into broad grins. We would have laughed out loud had we known how to laugh in a whisper.

"That's what happened," Barrio said. "Snoopy picked up the body heat of a bunch of monkeys, and we wasted a Arc Light raid on them. They won't replace us until they can tell the difference between NVA and monkeys."

After the mission I expecting some kind of formal evaluation of the job I had done. None was forthcoming, I learned that I had passed muster when my name appeared on the assignment board as Team Leader. My team continued to be Hotel Two Alpha. Barrio was temporarily assigned to BTOC, and I took over his call sign and team. To say I took over the team is a little misleading. For all intents and purposed the team was the team leader. All other members of the team were subject to change. In the fifteen missions I eventually ran as Team Leader I don't believe that I had exactly the same team on any two missions.

To have some cohesion, and to learn something about the men on my team I would often take them out to the trash dump and practice what we would do if we ran head on into the enemy. I would fire a magazine, peel off and retreat about fifteen yards. The RTO would then empty his magazine, then pull back behind me, then the third and forth man would do the same. By this time I would have reloaded, and we would repeat the process. It was a standard procedure for breaking contact, but I wanted to make sure that anybody on my team could handle it. I wanted to have a good team, and like many a coach believed in practicing the basics.

I soon developed the reputation of being a hard ass that would stand no nonsense on a mission. I had some set rules. My team ate cold rations. The smell of cooking food carried too far, and was too distinctive. As we were eating cold rations, we didn't need canteen cups, they were just another piece of metal to make noise. Team members had to carry at least twenty magazines for an M-16 or CAR-15, and they had to be carried in ammo, or canteen pouches. The bandoleers that a lot of GIs liked to wear around their chests tended to clank together when you took them off. They made too much noise.

I even banned the rubberized ponchos as too noisy, because they rustled when you wore them. That changed, however, after the monsoon season hit. After spending one mission soaked to the bone, and trying to sleep in a soaked poncho liner, the two square yards of shelter that the poncho provided from the torrential downpours, was sufficient justification for a little extra noise. I wasn't really a hard ass, I just wanted to bring my team back in one piece, and to survive Vietnam in the process.

My relations with Railwood didn't get any better once I was Team Leader. When he took over as acting Platoon Leader he decided to remake the platoon according to his vision of what a Ranger outfit should be, and that vision didn't include Spec. Four Team Leaders, especially those that hadn't been to school. He was a great believer in formal training. He gushed over people who had been to Ranger school in the States. If he couldn't get them, Recondo School graduates would do, but NCO school was a must.

I've told you that Railwood had refused to extract me when I was bitten by centipedes. But that wasn't our only run in. Early on I raised his ire by insisting on Radios that worked. The platoon's PRC-25s were old, and the batteries may have been even older. On two occasions I was given radios that worked in base camp, where Seven Niner Charley was only a few hundred yards away, but didn't work once we were in the field. Railwood, reluctantly, had to re-supply me in the field. Instead of scrounging for good radios, he put the word out that all teams would carry two radios, a radio to use, and a spare radio in case the first one didn't work.

In some instances he was even childish. On one visual reconnaissance we flew in a closed helicopter. I thought when we started out that it strange, this was the only time I had flown in a Huey with the cargo doors closed. It didn't take too long to figure out what he was up to. When we reached the AO instead of the wide circles, the pilot spiraled the ship down in ever tightening circles. In the closed confines of the bird my stomach began to churn. Railwood had apparently arranged it with the pilot to try to make me sick. I wouldn't give in though, I figured I could hold out as long as he could, and I did. When he saw I wasn't going to throw up, I'm sure his stomach was in no great shape either, he called off his game, and we returned to Mary Lou. I had survived, but I hadn't had an effective visual reconnaissance of the area. His childish prank could have put my team in danger.

When he recruited new LRPs he told them he was the Platoon Leader, but he never did officially assume that title. Hinkle told me that he was just holding it down till the brass could find someone who had more time in grade than he.

While Hinkle was there he could run interference, but in June of '69 Hinkle went home, and was replaced by Sergeant Hooper. Hooper was a good man and a good NCO, but he didn't challenge stupid orders from junior officers, and he didn't have Hinkle's pull with BTOC.

In early June my mother forwarded me a letter from Karen, and we reestablished our relationship through the mail. Up until then I hadn't thought much about going home. Now, I had a reason to look forward to it. By then too, I had well over the twenty-five missions that General Westmoreland had said was the upper demarcation of a LRP's effectiveness. I was starting to get a bit nervous, and was becoming overly cautious in the field. The fact was, I had now gone fifteen missions without a contact, and I was beginning to question whether I could handle it anymore. My In-Country R and R was coming up, and that would give me a break from running missions. I figured that with a bit or rest, I still had a few good missions left in me.

I was getting ready for that R and R when Sergeant Hooper came up to me.

"What do you think about Sergeant Hathaway? He's been your ATL on the last couple of missions." he asked.

"I like him," I said. "He may be the best ATL I've ever had assigned to me. He's not afraid to question decisions, and give me his opinion. That's what I need. It makes me think hard about the decisions I make, and sometimes I find that he has a good point. Sometimes we compromise, sometimes we do it his way, and sometimes I just explain what I'm trying to do a bit more clearly."

"Is he ready to be a Team Leader?"

"He's close," I said, "but there are a couple of things I'd like to teach him yet. Let me have him for a couple of more missions, and I'll give you a Team Leader to be proud of."

Hooper nodded his head.

26

Final Mission

Sunday June 21, 1969

Dear Diary,

The second out of country R and R promised when I signed up had long been forgotten by the brass. Now, like every other GI in Vietnam, a LRP gets one out of country, and one in-country R and R. For your in-country R and R you get three days in the sea side resort town of Vung Tau. The beaches were beautiful, the food was delicious, the booze was cheap, and the women were, for a price of course, willing. What more could a guy ask for?

More time out of action was the answer to that question. And I had the means of getting it. Genetics hadn't given me much to complain about. I was healthy and strong. Even though I had been thrown from horses, kicked by mules, and been involved in a couple of automobile accidents, I always seemed to walk away with no bones broken, and only a bruise or two to show for it. I did, however, inherit one genetic weakness, a predisposition to ingrown toenails. Usually I cut them out myself, but knowing I was going on R and R I let one continue to grow so that a visit to the doctor to have it removed would buy me a couple of more days out of the field. So, with two days for travel, three days in Vung Tau, and two more days in Pleiku for medical treatment, I was away from Mary Lou for a full week.

I returned in blissful ignorance of what had happened in my absence. I hitched a ride from the helicopter pad to the LRP cantonment in the back of a duce and a half, dropped my bag off at my tent, and was headed to the Headquarters tent to check in when I ran into Nesbit. Nesbit always knew what was going on in the platoon, and was a good source of information.

"What's up?" I said.

"Where have you been?" he said in a soft southern drawl.

"I just got back from my in-country R and R," I said. "I've been away for one full glorious week."

"Then you don't know what's been happening around here."

"I'm clueless," I said, "fill me in."

"We damn near lost a whole team while you were gone."

I was stunned, it had been more than a month since we'd had a contact. This might mean the start of a new offensive by the NVA.

"Who was it?" I asked.

"It was your old team, Hotel Two Alpha."

"My god," I said, "Who took my team? What happened?"

"Railwood recruited a new guy. An E-6 that had been to Ranger school in the states. He was checking out Hathaway to be a team leader. Evidently, when they hit the tree line the bad guys were already there, they ran into an ambush."

"Who else was on the Team? Are they ok?"

Nesbit held up his hand to slow me down. "Give me a minute, and I'll tell you. Hathaway is dead, he picked up a grenade that the gooks threw at them, and tried to throw it back. It blew up in his hand. It wounded the others too. The Staff Sergeant was bad enough to have to be sent back to the States."

"God, why didn't they listen to me? I told them that Hathaway wasn't ready, that he needed just a little more time."

"I have to hand it to Railwood, though," Nesbit said. "He showed real guts. He went in to the AO by himself, and found the guys, and he and one of the team that wasn't hurt as bad as the others, I think it was Misner, carried the E-6 back to the helicopter …"

"I never doubted Railwood's courage, just his sense."

"Anyway," Nesbit continued, "they went back and brought out Hathaway's body too."

That was all the information that Nesbit had, but gradually, from several sources, I learned the facts of the contact. Railwood had been the one pushing to make Hathaway a team leader. He selected the AO, and the LZ where they would be put in. There were two teams to be inserted that day, Hathaway and Hotel Two Alpha, and a team led by a LRP named Gallion. Hotel Two Alpha went in first. They hadn't even gotten to Gallion's AO before Hathaway reported movement. Railwood discounted the report, and continued with the insertion of the other team. The gunships stayed with Railwood to guard the second insertion. A second message from Hathaway reported that they were surrounded by the enemy.

They dropped off Gallion's team, making them jump rather than taking the time to land, and rushed back to where Hathaway had been inserted. By the time they arrived and the gunships started their run it was too late. Misner reported that the rest of the team were either dead or wounded. When the gunships ran out of ammunition Railwood took over, and directed artillery onto the area until a Forward Air control plane arrived on the scene. It was then that Railwood went in, armed only with a 45 automatic.

He did indeed show courage, but I couldn't help but wonder what would have happened if he had returned at the team's first call, if the gunships had gotten there earlier, if he had been able to lead in another full LRP team to aid their comrades. Would Hathaway have been saved? Would they have been able to fight off the enemy, or would two teams have been destroyed? I will never know, I only know what he didn't do.

The next time that Hotel Two Alpha appeared on the scheduling board I was once again listed as Team Leader. The other members of the team were new to me, I hadn't run missions with any of them. The ATL that was assigned to me was Hardin. Plant, and Howell were snipers, specially trained and armed with scoped, match grade M-14s. The only problem was that those M-14s fired only semi-automatic. I should have expected that at some point I would have to take out snipers. The Hotel designation in Hotel Two Alpha stood for Hawkeye, or according to some, hunter killer. In either case, it meant teams designated to ambush the enemy rather than just perform reconnaissance. In the past I had set up ambushes on likely looking trails, but it had only been as the opportunity afforded itself. I had never been ordered to set up an ambush, and I had never been assigned snipers.

"There's something I should tell you about this team," Sergeant Hooper said. "All three have been rejected by two other team leaders." There was a rule among the LRPs that if someone was rejected by three team leaders they were out of the outfit.

"I don't know anything about Hardin," I said, "but I know Plant and Howell. They've been around for a few months and they don't seem to be bad Lerps."

"Their rejections have come since they returned from sniper school. My guess is that it's their M-14s that are being rejected."

"Semi-automatics do cut down on your ability to lay down a blanket of fire," I said. To myself I wondered if Howell hadn't been rejected because he was black.

The LRPs were like a microcosm of America, we had blacks, whites, Latinos, Indians, and, unfortunately, even the occasional bigot.

"What about Hardin?" I asked.

"They didn't say when they rejected him, I guess they just don't like him."

"I seem to have gotten more than my share of rejects of late."

"That's because you don't reject them, you're willing to train them and work with them. Some of us think you're a good teacher, and can bring them around. Others just think you're an easy mark. In either case it means that we can keep the roster full, and don't have to recruit new LRPs."

Ironically, it would not be the team members of Hotel Two Alpha that were in danger of being kicked out of the LRPs; it would be the Team Leader. The first hint of what was to come came during the insertion flight. In front of the entire team Railwood leaned over and pointed at my Swedish K.

"There's rust on that weapon soldier," he said. "You should take better care of Government property."

I looked down on my sub-machine gun. There was a spot of rust no bigger than the head of a pin on one of the rivets. "I assure you, Sir, the shooting end is perfectly clean. Would you like to inspect that part of the weapon?" There was the hint of a threat in my voice.

"It's too late for that now," Railwood said, missing, or ignoring the point of my invitation. "Just see you do better in the future."

A few minutes later we were jumping from the skids of the hovering helicopter into the LZ. It didn't seem to be an appropriate AO for snipers. The sniper rifles were accurate up to one mile, but this AO didn't have any locations where you could see for a mile. Even though there was a lot of open grassland there were no promontories, not even any tall trees. It was one of those unusual areas in the Central Highlands that was mostly elephant grass with only a few patches of jungle. But, it was here we would spend the next three nights and four days. We began to explore.

For now I will withhold what happened during that mission, but be patient, in time I will tell the whole story. Suffice it to say that it caused me to remember a conversation I had with Shaner some nine months earlier. He had just told me that he had nearly forty missions when he stopped going to the field.

"Why did you quit?" I had asked.

"You know when it's time," he told me. Nine months and thirty-four missions later, I knew that it was my time.

The last morning of the mission was windy. I had brought a paper back book with me that was not well made. Some of the pages came loose, and blew around the night location. Before I could pick them up the radio crackled with word that the extraction ships were on the way. I had been told not to expect extraction until the afternoon. The early extraction came out of the blue. There was no time to run down the pages, we had to pack up and find a good place for the choppers to land ASAP. We gathered our gear stuffed them into our packs, rolled our poncho liners and secured them to the bottom of the packs and headed into the elephant grass to clear a landing area.

We had cleared an area just big enough to be seen by the helicopter when we heard the whirring of the rotor blades. Following the instructions of the pilot I popped smoke, and he identified the color. As he began to make his landing pass the spinning blades revealed that the area was not as clear as we had thought. The stalks of a half dozed charred trees appeared like natures pungy stakes ready to snare the approaching chopper. The area was dotted with the remnants of a past fire, hidden by the elephant grass until the prop wash revealed its menacing presence.

"We can push some of them down," I told the pilot over the radio.

"Negative," he replied, "there's a small stream about sixty meters north, head there, and we'll pick you up out of the water."

"Roger," I said. Pointing toward the stream I told the team, "head that way to the creek they'll pick us up there."

The helicopter arrived ahead of us, and was hovering a couple of feet above the water. The water was knee deep, which made the skids chest high. With the extra weight of packs and gear it was a struggle to get on board. I gave the team members a leg up then they pulled me up until I could get a foot on a skid. Finally we were on board, and the chopper rose up, did a 180 degree turn and headed back for Mary Lou.

Once we had landed we piled our packs into the little wagon hitched behind the jeep, and climbed into the back of the jeep. Railwood, who had flown in the chase helicopter, climbed in beside Cueball.

"That's one hell of a mess you made in that night location," he said, turning to me. "The AO is compromised, they'll know we've been there."

I didn't answer him directly, "I need out of the field," I said. "I can't do this anymore."

"You're not getting out that easy, soldier," he said scowling. "You'll be out there again, but with a bunch of grunts. I'm going to see you're drummed out of the Rangers and sent to a line unit. If I could order it done, I would, but we've got a new Platoon Leader now, and I'm going to have to tell him about your screw up, and let him do it."

So they had finally found somebody with more time in grade than he had, I thought. I would say no more to Railwood, there could be no fair hearing from him. As it turned out, the officer they found not only had more time in grade, but was a lot more open minded than Railwood. He wasn't going to hang me on Railwood's word alone, he was going to look into the situation.

Lieutenant Street, the new Platoon Leader, began to investigate Railwood's charges against me almost immediately. He talked to others first. He talked to the other members of my team, he talked to Sergeant Hopper, he even talked to Major McIntosh. Finally he called for me to come to the Headquarters tent.

I entered the tent and stood before his desk. He still wore regular green jungle fatigues. He had curly hair and strong features, and was about my own age.

"Lieutenant Railwood thinks you should be dropped from the Lerp platoon, and sent to a line unit." He spoke in a soft non-distinct voice. "He said you compromised a potentially valuable area of operations by leaving a considerable amount of trash in your night location. What have you to say for yourself?"

"I brought a book along on the mission. I had laid it down that morning when I was taking my canteen out of my pack. It was windy, and the binding of the book was weak, a dozen or so pages blew out. I was about to pick them up when we got word that the helicopters were on their way. We had no prior warning, and weren't expecting extraction until the afternoon."

"Why didn't you go ahead and pick them up?"

"There wasn't time. The whole area was covered by elephant grass, and I thought we would have to knock out an area where the chopper could see us. As it turned out there were too many burned out trees that were hidden by the elephant grass. The chopper couldn't land, and the pilot had to direct us to a nearby creek."

"Then the helicopters arrived before you had time to clean up the area?"

"Yes sir."

"You told Lieutenant Railwood that you wanted out of the Lerps?"

"No sir, I told him I wanted out of the field. I'm getting dangerous out there."

"Because you leave papers lying around?"

"No sir, the only thing those pages would do in the unlikely event that they were ever found by the NVA, would be to make them waste time trying to figure out who Nero Wolf and Archie Goodwin are, and what they have to do with the Americans in Vietnam." The Lieutenant actually cracked a smile.

"I'm dangerous because of what happened on the second night of the mission," I said. "Our night location was in the middle of the elephant grass. It seemed like a pretty safe area. We squeezed into the grass, and replaced all the broken blades with grass from the inside. Then we moved further into the grass about forty or fifty yards, and made our night location.

"We began running watches at 2100 hours and continued them for nine hours, until 600 hours in the morning. I always take the first and last watch myself. Each of us stands watch for an hour. You can stay awake for an hour, but if you try to go for two or three hours, you run the risk of falling asleep on watch. That means that each of my team members gets two one hour stints on watch and I get three. By taking the last watch from 500 to 600 hours, I'm awake at daylight and can call in the sunshine report. I finished my first watch at 2200 hours and woke up Plant who had the next watch. Then I rolled up in my poncho liner, and went to sleep.

"At some point I rolled over on my back. I remember it was a full moon, or near a full moon that night. It was almost as light as it had been at dusk. It was then that I saw the elephant grass in front of me part, and a figure step into our night location. I could see his pith helmet, and make out the details of his North Vietnamese uniform. He pulled an AK-47 from behind him brought it to his shoulder, and aimed it right at me. I sat up, and told Plant 'Shoot him! Shoot him!'

"Then Plant shook me—and it wasn't bright, the moon wasn't even up yet, and there was nobody there but us. I had dreamed the whole thing."

"So you were scared," Street said. "Haven't you been scared before?"

"Of course I've been scared before, scared you deal with every day. Scared is when S-2 tells you that there will a battalion of North Vietnamese crossing the area you are going into, and that he wants you and three other men to find them. Scared is after you've been in a fire fight, and you look down and see that all the grass around you is torn up by bullet and shrapnel holes. Scared is when you look down at the dead body of a man you killed, and know that body could just as easily have been yours. Scared is all around you, and you deal with it—but talking out loud in your sleep, that you can't deal with. You can't stop dreaming, and you can't control what you dream, and when it causes you to talk out loud you don't put just yourself in danger, but you risk the lives of your entire team."

"So, you're telling me that you want out because you're a danger to your team?"

"My job for you is to find out what's out there, my job for them is to bring them home alive."

Lieutenant Street sat quietly for a minute tapping the eraser of a pencil on the desk. "I want you to talk to a psychiatric officer," he said finally. "I think you've been out there long enough, but I want him to confirm it."

"I'll do whatever you say, sir."

When I left the tent I found Howell waiting for me.

"I told the Lieutenant they can't do this to you," he said. "I told him that you were the best Team Leader I've ever gone out there with. Plant said the same thing, we said that you were one of the giants of this outfit, that treating you this way was wrong."

I wanted to tell him that I wasn't a giant, that Titans were a myth, and that we were all just men who were trying to survive out there. But, I couldn't. He needed giants, and Plant needed giants, at one time or another we all needed giants. Howell and Plant needed me as I had needed Festus, and Colbray, and Miller. The giants were our mentors, our role models, living examples of how to survive the insanity of war. They were the men that had been there and done that, and lived to tell about it. They were still only men perhaps, but to the FNG in all of us they were giants. I couldn't deny him his giants, all I could say was, "thanks man, I really appreciate it."

Railwood lost. I ended my time in Vietnam as I had started, as a LRP. Except for Railwood himself, the testimony had all been in my favor. It seems even Major Macintosh stood up for me. The psychiatrist said that my dream was caused by a mild case of combat fatigue and that I needed a rest. A couple of days later Lieutenant Street called me back up to the Headquarters Tent.

"You're returning to K Company 75th Infantry Rangers," he told me. "They have an opening for Company Armorer that they want you to fill."

"Thank you Sir." As I turned to go I thought of something else. "Sir, the Swedish K that I carried for the last twenty some missions is in the conex. I know that I can't take it with me to Pleiku, but it has been a good weapon, and I'd like it to go to somebody who would appreciate it. I'd like you to have it if you're interested."

"Thank you, Reed, I'll have a look at it," he said.

I arrived at K-75th before the end of the second week in July. I was on duty in the supply tent when on July 14th I heard the words, "Tranquility Base here the Eagle has landed," and mankind set down on the surface of the moon. On the 29th of July Neugard came to Pleiku, and we both participated in a ceremony awarding us Air Medals for participating in more than twenty five aerial missions, and Army Commendation Medals for our service as LRP Team Leaders. I had been right, I didn't need a ceremony, but it felt damned good to be appreciated.

On September 17, 1969 Karen met me at the Kansas City airport. I was home.

Epilogue

I looked at my audience, there were veterans of both World Wars there, they at least understood my feelings on that night, that night when the world was crashing around the people of South Vietnam. I resumed speaking.

"But the saddest of all my memories are of those courageous Americans who fought and all too often died there. Here the memories are more personal. From the dim past I see vague reflections of familiar faces; I hear a roll call of names long since forgotten by the conscious mind. Names like Finley, and Gahati and Murphy and Hancock and Blake, and Hathaway, city boys and country boys, whites and blacks and even an American Indian, College grads and high school dropouts; in one unit a microcosm of American life.

"Finley has been missing in action since November 1968; the others are dead, killed in action in an undeclared and unpopular war. But perhaps I'm wrong, perhaps death is more ephemeral than I know. Jerry Hancock thought it was. Jerry wrote poetry and I fought beside him over there. On occasion he would let me read some of his poems. After the helicopter he was on went down killing him and his entire team we found this poem among his effects, I have since learned it wasn't one he had written, but none the less it reflected his beliefs. The lieutenant read it during the ceremony awarding him a Bronze Star and Purple Heart posthumously.

> "Do not stand by my grave and weep,
> I am not there, I do not sleep.
> I am a thousand winds that blow,
> I am the diamond glints on the snow,
> I am the sunlight on ripening grain,
> I am the gentle autumn rain.
> When you wake in the morning hush
> I am the swift uplifting rush
> of birds in winged flight
> I am the soft starshine at night.
> Do not stand by my grave and cry
> I am not there, I did not die."

I remember Vietnam, I remember the Vietnamese people, but most of all I remember Jerry, and Finley and Gahati and Murphy and Hathaway and the rest."

I sat down there was no more to say.

978-0-595-42372-9
0-595-42372-8

Printed in the United States
152239LV00002B/67/A